To Luiz

I want to thank my dear friend, Luiz
Hara, who has been supporting my
cookery courses over the years. As well
as his full time investment bank job,
Luiz runs an extremely popular food
blog called 'The London Foodie'. I first
met Luiz in my Sushi and Sashimi class
back in 2005; he had come back for
various courses I was offering at the
time. Luiz kindly tells me that he has
enjoyed every single course he has taken
and has consequently gained a true
understanding and appreciation of
Japanese food. When I receive this kind
of comment from my students, it does
make me realise how lucky I am to be
doing what I do. I am extremely grateful
to have met Luiz and to be able to share
and exchange our knowledge of food.
I feel very lucky to have such a precious
friend who has faith in my food and
supports my work. Thank you, Luiz.

REIKO HASHIMOTO

HASHI

A JAPANESE COOKERY COURSE

ABSOLUTE PRESS **A.**

Durham County Council
Libraries, Learning
and Culture

C0 1 70 53244 5B	
Askews & Holts	
641.5952	

First published in Great Britain
in 2011 by
Absolute Press
Scarborough House
29 James Street West
Bath BA1 2BT
Phone 44 (0) 1225 316013
Fax 44 (0) 1225 445836
E-mail info@absolutepress.co.uk
Website www.absolutepress.co.uk

Text © Reiko Hashimoto
Photography © Mike Cooper
(except cover montage images from
Fotolia.com: 'alte papier'
© suzannmeer; and 'red fabric
background' © Freesurf, both of
which also appear inside this book)

Publisher Jon Croft
Commissioning Editor Meg Avent
Art Direction & Design Matt Inwood
Design Assistant Claire Siggery

Editor Anne Sheasby
Photographer Mike Cooper
Food Stylist Reiko Hashimoto

ISBN 9781906650575

A catalogue record of this book is
available from the British Library.

The rights of Reiko Hashimoto to
be identified as the author of this
work have been asserted by her
in accordance with the Copyright
Designs and Patents Act 1988.

All rights reserved. No part of this
publication may be reproduced,
stored in a retrieval system or
transmitted in any form or by any
means, electronic or otherwise,
without the prior permission of
Absolute Press.

Printed and bound on behalf of
Latitude Press in Slovenia.

A note about the text
This book is set in Minion, Helvetica
Neue and Sabon MT. Minion was
created by Robert Slimbach,
inspired by fonts of the late
Renaissance. Helvetica was
designed in 1957 by Max Miedinger
of the Swiss-based Haas foundry.
In the early 1980s, Linotype redrew
the entire Helvetica family. The
result was Helvetica Neue. Sabon
was designed by Jan Tschichold in
1964. The roman design is based
on type by Claude Garamond,
whereas the italic design is based
on types by Robert Granjon.

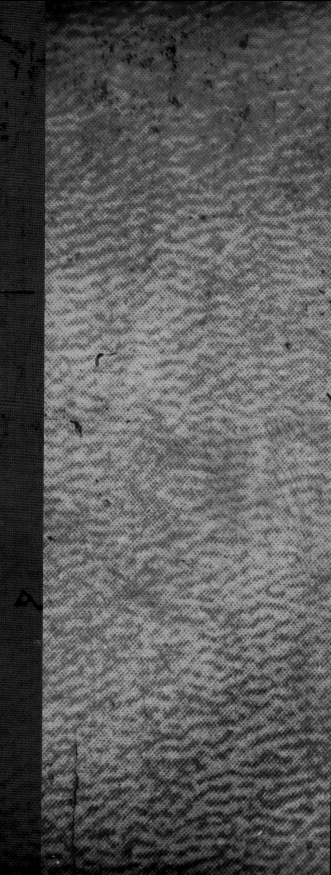

CONTENTS

ABOUT THE AUTHOR

Reiko Hashimoto has been teaching Japanese cooking for over 12 years. In that time, she has set thousands of students on the path to creative and accessible Japanese cooking. Now she has the pleasure of sharing her culinary secrets with you.

Reiko was born in Kyoto, the ancient capital of Japan. She grew up in a traditional Japanese family with a food-fanatic mother who has shaped her love of Japanese cooking today.

After studying English Literature at university, Reiko started work as an airhostess and was based in Hong Kong, a real foodie's paradise. Travelling around the world with her airline broadened Reiko's understanding and interest in food from all corners of the globe. After leaving the airline, Reiko decided to make a career from cooking and teaching, by introducing Japanese cuisine to her foreign friends living in Japan.

Reiko then moved to London and set up a company called 'HASHI' to cater for Japanese dinner parties – from formal sit-down dinner parties to casual canapé parties. A lot of the people Reiko catered for asked if she could teach them how to cook, and so Reiko then decided to also teach Japanese cooking.

So, for nearly 10 years, Reiko has been teaching people the joy of Japanese cooking, coaching them from raw beginners to cordon bleu-level chefs. She has appeared on television many times and has been featured on programmes such as Good Food Live and The Great British Kitchen as a guest chef. She has also been featured in numerous magazine articles.

To many, Reiko is the acknowledged expert in Japanese cooking in the UK. And now she has taken her love of Japanese food one step further by producing this beautifully presented definitive book on how to cook Japanese food at home.

FOREWORD

I was very fortunate to be brought up in a family that always had freshly cooked meals prepared by my mother who was very keen on fresh flavours and very fresh food. I remember waking up every morning and going downstairs to the sound of a shaving noise in the kitchen. Mother was shaving the solid dried and smoked bonito fish to make the flakes for dashi stock. Not only did she make the stock from scratch each morning – most Japanese people buy bonito flakes already shaven and use sea kelp (konbu or kombu) to make fresh stock – but she actually shaved the fish every morning to obtain the freshest bonito flakes to simply make the miso soup for our breakfast.

Now, most people use an instant dashi stock powder to make the soup, which is tasty enough, but if you were brought up with the real fresh flavour it is very difficult to accept these quicker, more modern alternatives. That's where my belief for the true flavours comes from.

I was also fortunate to be born and grow up in Kyoto where we always had an abundance of seasonal mountain vegetables. The important thing about Japanese food is that you very much rely on fresh seasonal ingredients to achieve the best flavours. As we have four distinct seasons in Japan, what we see in the supermarkets each season differs to reflect what is grown and available at that time of year. I try to go back to see my parents in Kyoto once a year and choose to be there in either spring or autumn, as these two seasons often have the most beautiful ingredients and weather.

For example, in the early spring, you will see freshly picked bamboo shoots, called Takenoko, in any supermarket, local grocery shop and of course in the food hall of the department store. The texture of takenoko is quite similar to a good quality, fresh artichoke. You simply boil the bamboo shoots first, then peel, cut and simmer them with a very subtle broth based on fresh dashi stock and a little soy sauce. This dish is often cooked with fresh wakame seaweed. We can buy dried wakame seaweed here in the UK, but sadly it is nothing like the fresh wakame that we can get in Japan. Takenoko delivers a combination of nutty and woody flavours with a crunchy texture, making it absolutely unforgettable and addictive.

In the autumn, you will see these shockingly priced but ordinary-looking mushrooms everywhere in Japan. They are called Matsutake. I can only afford to cook these mushrooms just once during my stay, but it is well worth going to Japan in the autumn just for this, especially if you are a foodie. As you approach a shop that sells matsutake, you start getting the deep earthy mushroom scent, which you may have experienced with truffles. However, this Japanese version of truffles is very firm in texture and looks a little bit like a giant shiitake mushroom with a much thicker stem. The most popular way to cook matsutake is to simply slice them thinly and simmer in fresh dashi stock with a small amount of leafy vegetables. A little seasoning is required to bring out the wonderfully fresh and earthy flavours of the mushrooms and they are served simply with fresh Yuzu (Japanese lime) on the side. I am almost salivating at the thought! However, my favourite way is to cook matsutake on the grill (preferably over charcoal), then serve them dipped in a little soy sauce and a squeeze of yuzu – heavenly!

Not surprisingly, I believe in authentic flavours and that is where my true love of food is based.

JAPANESE FOOD CULTURE

THE BENEFITS OF JAPANESE FOOD – LIVE LONG, STAY SLIM AND PROSPER

Japan has one of the highest life expectancies in the world and has held the highest life expectancy record for decades. On average, Japanese women live to be over 86 years old and Japanese men live to almost 80 years old. There are two reasons for this – one is the advanced medical treatment we receive and the other, undoubtedly, is the diet.

Typically, Japanese meals consist of many small dishes with a variety of different textures and ingredients, eaten very slowly. Most Japanese people tend to eat less meat and dairy products compared to the Western diet and take their protein mostly from fish, soya beans and seeds. Oily fish is eaten daily by most Japanese people and that, it is believed, has led to the fact that very few elderly Japanese people suffer from joint problems. Japanese people consume the most fish per person and catch the most variety of fish in the world.

The staple Japanese ingredients of miso and soy sauce are both fermented soya bean products that are rich in protein, vitamins and minerals, which are good and important nutrients for the human body. Both miso and soy sauce are high in natural sodium (salt), which is why very little added salt is used in Japanese cooking.

Naturally, I'm a great believer in a good balanced diet, which leads to happiness, good concentration and an active lifestyle.

WHY ARE JAPANESE PEOPLE SO SLIM?

One obvious thing I notice whenever I go back to Japan – having now lived in the UK for over 12 years – is that Japanese people are so slim by comparison. You don't often see fat people in Japan (even the sumo wrestlers gorge themselves to make themselves fat!) though you sometimes see slightly overweight people. So what makes us so slim?

The Japanese diet is reasonably high in carbohydrate but the fat content is extremely low compared to the typical Western diet. Indeed, the Japanese diet seems to be at odds with the (once) fashionable low-carb diet. You may lose a large amount of weight quite quickly by not eating starchy carbohydrates, but generally the human body requires carbohydrates to help it to absorb all the other nutrients. Most Japanese/Asian people have starchy carbohydrates in each meal along with many small dishes and that keeps their diet well-balanced. It has also been proven that if you take your time eating, then you will eat less. Japanese food is typically served in many small dishes that are served well spaced out. Another reason is very little animal fat is used in Japanese food, including the traditional Japanese desserts. Although you see many Western fast food chains and pretty French patisseries in Japan these days (and many young people frequently visit those places), the basic cooking methods remain as the traditional ways taught at home. Therefore most Japanese people generally crave for less fat and less rich food. If you try MacDonald's or KFC in Japan, you will notice they produce food that is much less fatty and greasy than the equivalents in the West.

The Japanese diet is heavy on vegetables and fish and light on meat, the missing protein being replaced by soya products such as the many varieties of tofu. These soya products are much lower in calories and are highly nutritious, which is perfect for an everyday diet.

Another ingredient often used in Japanese cooking is seaweed. The most commonly used stock is made with dried bonito flakes and sea kelp (konbu or kombu). We have many varieties of

seaweed in Japan. A few of them have travelled over here to the UK and are becoming quite popular. You can obtain these seaweeds from health food stores or even local supermarkets these days.

SEASONAL (SHUN) AND REGIONAL FOOD (KYODO RYO-RI)

There are four distinct seasons in Japan. Each season lasts for about three months and produces different types of fresh produce to be used alongside the vegetables produced in greenhouses and the farmed fish, available all year round. In Japanese cooking, the use of seasonal produce is paramount and is called Shun. When people cook a meal, it is common practice to use shun ingredients. In general, shun food represents fish, vegetables and fruits.

Japan consists of four main islands. The northern island is called Hokkaido, the main island is called Honshu, then we have Shikoku and finally the southern island which is called Kyushu. These

four islands stretch from Russia right through to South Korea. The north side of Japan is facing the Japanese Sea and the other side is facing the Pacific Ocean. The difference in the sea's currents and temperatures attract many varieties of fish.

Japan is also a country formed with huge inhabitable mountains running through the centre of the land from the north to the south. This is why Japan is one of the most highly-densely populated countries in the world, as people tend to live within the 20–25% non-mountainous areas. These solid mountains also make both of the sea's currents rather unique and this leads to Japan having access to one of the

largest variety of fish and shellfish in the world.

These geographical factors create not only an abundance of fish but also an abundance of vegetables. The combination of the altitude of the mountains, the humidity we experience and the different temperatures of the four distinct seasons, creates the variety of vegetables and mountain vegetables of each season. Japanese people are mushroom lovers as well as lovers of fish. In recent years, we have started to see Japanese mushrooms outside of Japan and they have proven to be very popular.

THE IMPORTANCE OF PRESENTATION WITH JAPANESE FOOD

One of the reasons why sushi has become so popular is because of its beautiful appearance. Generally speaking, Japanese people take really good care over the presentation of food,

even in their daily family meals. Indeed, some people regard Japanese food as a work of art. Just a little extra care in slicing the food (with a sharp knife) to produce the straight, sharp cut line, or

chopping the vegetables finely, helps to make each dish look very elegant. We also think about the colour and texture combinations of the food.

You may like to invest in some Japanese crockery so that you can present your dishes in such a way to enhance the pleasure of dining. Japanese dinner service (crockery) is unlike Western or Chinese crockery that typically uses a set of matching designs for the entire meal. Japanese tend to use a variety of plates and bowls for each course/dish.

They are a different texture, colour and shape and are chosen to go with each dish.

One pair of chopsticks is used throughout the meal except for dessert. Japanese chopsticks have a narrow end towards the bottom and are traditionally made from wood. Chinese chopsticks have no narrow end and are traditionally made from ivory-like material, but tend to be made of plastic these days. Japanese usually place chopsticks horizontally and close to you, with the chopsticks rest placed on the left where the narrow end is (as it is considered that you are a right-handed person). Chinese chopsticks are placed vertically on your right side.

JAPANESE FOOD – UNDERSTANDING THE BASIC ETIQUETTE

Whenever you go somewhere with a different culture and eat food with the locals you may quite inadvertently be doing something that is rude or offensive to these people. I don't want to alarm you too much as Japanese people are generally very accepting towards non-Japanese people. However, it is useful to know the general etiquette and if you do follow these basic etiquette guidelines, you will receive a great deal of appreciation in return.

It is well-mannered to show respect by saying *Itadaki-Masu* before picking up chopsticks. Similarly, you should finish a meal by saying *Gachiso-Sama* accompanied by a little bow to your fellow diners. There is no exact translation for these words in English as these short words include so many meanings. If I were to explain them in simple, literal English, they would mean 'I will graciously receive and enjoy the meal' and 'I thank for the precious meal that I was given'.

If the food is served like a small buffet-style selection on the table, and a serving spoon or separate chopsticks are not provided, use the reverse end of your chopsticks to pick the food from the shared plate, thus avoiding any 'contamination' of the food from one diner to another.

When you are not using chopsticks, you must always rest the chopsticks laying horizontally on the chopsticks rest.

Never pass food with chopsticks. Always pass the plate or bowl to fellow diners to allow them to help themselves.

Leaving rice, even one grain, is considered to be impolite. The Japanese staple diet is rice and people are supposed to show respect to farmers who provide the staple food. So make sure you eat that last grain of rice from now on!

When eating sushi or sashimi, do not mix the wasabi paste into soy sauce to spice up the sauce. This is considered to be rude to the chef as it kills the flavour of the fresh ingredients. Soy sauce is used only as a seasoning rather than as a sauce, and wasabi is a condiment, so a small amount of each with each mouthful is appropriate.

When eating sushi, do not fill up to the top of the soy sauce plate with soy sauce. Try dipping the sushi with only a little bit of soy sauce. If it is a hand-moulded piece of sushi (nigiri), try dipping the fish side rather than the rice in the sauce, so that the rice will not break up and you will have a clear soy sauce until the end of your meal.

When someone is pouring drinks for you, it is courteous to hold or raise your cup/glass up to receive the drink (rather than to leave the cup/glass on the table while the drink is being poured). If you

HASHI

are a woman, you need to hold the cup/glass with both hands. Once you have received your drink, you are then expected in return to pour the sake for the person who has just poured your drink. Again, if you are a woman, when pouring the sake, you also need to hold the bottle with both hands.

Mind you, it should also be said that some Japanese eating habits cause concern to Westerners. For example, our habit of slurping our noodles to show how much we enjoy it is rather frowned upon here!

TEACHING JAPANESE COOKERY

I have been running Japanese cookery courses in London for nearly 10 years and I have learnt that it is very important to go through the stages, step by step. No matter how experienced and how great a cook or chef you are, if you haven't done Japanese cooking, you are still a novice in this cuisine. However, let me assure you that you will learn quickly by following the various stages set out in this book.

In my cookery school, I run Beginners, Home Cooking, Gourmet and Master Chef courses alongside Sushi and Sashimi classes. When people first enquire about taking a course, I usually recommend that they take the Beginners course first, unless they are familiar with using all the basic Japanese ingredients.

The Beginners course is like a foundation course that gives you a good understanding of the ingredients and flavours in Japanese food. By the end of the four sessions, people are normally quite confident with using the basic Japanese ingredients and have developed the right palate. This is what I'm trying to help everyone to achieve by using this book. Fundamentally, I have structured this book in the same way that I have structured my courses, i.e. a chapter for Beginners, a chapter on Home Cooking and a chapter on Gourmet Cooking. Towards the end, there is a chapter on Sushi, followed by a final chapter on Desserts.

Once you have grasped the basic understanding of both familiar and well-known Japanese dishes (Beginners Chapter, pages 41–87), you will move on to how Japanese families really eat every day – basically comfort food and home-cooked dishes (Home Cooks Chapter, pages 89–137). This chapter may well be the most exciting part amongst true Japanese food lovers. Many dishes in this chapter don't even have Japanese names, but are utterly delicious, unpretentious and down-to-earth.

In the next section (Gourmet Chapter, pages 139–183), the climax of this book shows you how you can create a sophisticated Japanese dinner party at home. This includes guidance on not only how to prepare and cook the dishes, but also on the presentation of the finished dishes and the simplest way of achieving all this.

These first three sections are organised in a standard order and include Soups and Starters, Salads and Side Dishes, Fish and Seafood, Meat and Poultry, Rice and Noodles, and finally, Tofu.

There's also a separate chapter containing basic recipes that are used repeatedly throughout the book, such as sauces, stocks, rice, etc. As you make use of this book, you will eventually be able to create these basic sauces and stocks without the recipes.

USING THIS BOOK

Some people think that Japanese food is an expensive taste to acquire and this attitude has been partly fostered by the growing number of chic new Japanese eateries that cater for London's expense-account diners. This book challenges this expensive myth by demonstrating how a complete beginner can prepare a delicious Japanese meal (sometimes in under 20 minutes) with economical ingredients from a local supermarket, for typically less than £5 per head! A similar meal from a Japanese restaurant may well cost you around £40 per head, so in these austere times, my book can help lovers of Japanese food save a lot of money, whilst enjoying Japanese food in the comfort of their home.

The aim of this book is to introduce you to some of the different types of Japanese cooking. Like any other cuisine, we have everyday dishes, celebration dishes, sophisticated restaurant dishes and so on.

This book is for everyone. For the curious beginner, it offers reassuring confidence. For the seasoned expert, it is an advanced master-class. Everything is explained in clear and simple language. This is genuinely a cookery book for all abilities – you just need to be an inspired Japanese food lover!

Japanese store cupboard ingredients are few and simple, as with Italian cooking. We use a limited number of ingredients repeatedly. In many respects, it is more difficult to create a distinct flavour when you use a few herbs and ingredients. Because of this, the quality of ingredients is very important, more so than with any other cuisine. Also, the timing and the temperature of the cooking are very important for Japanese cooking. You will gradually learn all of this by following the recipes in this book.

BEGINNERS – AUTHENTIC AND EASY-TO-PREPARE DISHES

Most of the dishes in this section are well known and easy-to-prepare dishes for the novice. You will probably already know what many of the dishes should look and taste like and that will instantly make you feel more comfortable and will help you to cook with confidence. Indeed, this chapter will help to demystify Japanese cooking altogether!

I have selected the dishes that use easily obtained ingredients from your local supermarket, as well as the basic store cupboard ingredients. This makes it easier for you to get started. Once you have cooked your way through this chapter, you will be surprised just how simple it is to cook Japanese food at home.

HOME COOKING – LOW BUDGET AND COMFORT FOOD

You will see many dishes in this section that you may not have heard of nor seen before. Many of these dishes are eaten on a daily basis in Japanese homes. They may not win prizes for their appearance, but they are high in nutrients, economical and most of all, very tasty – perfect comfort food.

These dishes are ideal if you are expecting many hungry visitors. You can serve them as a buffet meal and they will not blow your budget. My two sons are currently at university and they come home more often than everybody else (so they say) simply because they miss the home cooking dishes which are introduced in this chapter.

GOURMET – BEAUTIFUL AND SOPHISTICATED

In this section, I show you some sophisticated and beautiful dishes, which you would typically see in upmarket Japanese restaurants. The ingredients are generally pricey and are not always easy to get hold of but the dishes are well worth the effort!

The techniques required are not necessarily too complicated, but you need to have a thorough understanding of the ingredients to appreciate the expensive ones, hence the timing, temperature and method of cooking are important factors when cooking these dishes. Let's not forget about the presentation as well. I include useful tips on how the food should be presented so that you can soon start hosting posh dinner parties at home!

SUSHI – JAPAN'S NATIONAL DISH

Sushi is Japan's national dish. It has the longest history amongst all the Japanese dishes and there are many different varieties of sushi depending on the region, the season and the occasion.

Sushi was first founded back in the 7th century in China. Originally sushi was a way of preserving fish by using salt and rice to ferment the fish; the rice was then discarded. This method has been traced back to South East Asian countries and it still remains one of the best ways of preserving food. Eventually, during the 14th century, vinegar was added to the mixture for a better taste and a better way of preserving. Oshi-zushi (compressed sushi) was created with rice, salt, vinegar and fish, and was founded in Osaka. Vinegar keeps the fish preserved for a longer period and gives it a better flavour. The contemporary version of this is called nigiri (hand-moulded sushi) and was created in 1800 in 'Edo' (the old name for Tokyo). That is why nigiri can be called Edo-Mae Nigiri-Zushi. In those days, nigiri was only eaten in the Tokyo area using fish that was caught locally. However, in 1923, many sushi chefs lost their job due to the Great Kanto Earthquake disaster and had to travel to find a job elsewhere. Thus, nigiri was then made all over Japan.

There are only a few limited kinds of sushi eaten outside of Japan that tend to appeal more to the non-Japanese palate, but the popularity of sushi is greater now than ever before, so a better selection is gradually becoming more widely available. People have become much more health-conscious and therefore enjoy the fact that sushi is low in fat, it is a source of many good nutrients and is very light. For example, a typical sushi meal is around 400–500 kilocalories and contains many healthy elements such as protein, omega-3 fatty acids and amino acids. The only negative element of sushi is the amount of sugar in the sushi vinegar, but you can control this when you make sushi at home. It's time to move from the Atkins to the new wave of Sushi diet!

One slight drawback with eating sushi in the West is that if you want to eat top quality sushi in a restaurant, you need to have a healthy income, as it is rare to find it at low prices. However, if you follow the advice given in this book, you can now make sushi at home relatively cheaply. I include several varieties of sushi, from the more traditional ones to the modern fusion styles, all explained step by step, so that there won't be any confusion.

DESSERTS – JAPAN MEETS FRANCE

Lastly, you will see a small section on desserts. I did question myself as to whether or not I should include desserts in this book. Traditional Japanese sweets are considered artistic and detailed. They are often made with rare ingredients, which are difficult to find outside of Japan and unfortunately, the flavours are often not appreciated by the Western palate. Also, a lot of time and effort are involved, which can be quite off-putting. But I thought that no cookery book is complete unless it has some desserts in it, so I relented.

I have created a few fusion Japanese desserts whilst maintaining the use of basic Japanese ingredients. As the Japanese love French desserts, the Japanese/French fusion has almost become the default Japanese dessert for the younger generation, at least nowadays. Try my versions of these Japanese/French fusion desserts and see if they appeal to you. They may not be very authentic but I guarantee they are Japanese in essence and are very tasty.

EQUIPMENT AND UTENSILS

KNIVES (HOCHO)
There are many types of knives in the Japanese kitchen. The all-purpose knife is the most commonly used one in the domestic kitchen, whereas in the professional kitchen, between ten and fifteen different knives may be used. It is always important to keep knives sharp and to sharpen them with a stone sharpener.

RICE COOKER (SUIHANKI)
You can cook rice in a heavy-based pan, but if you eat rice at least once or twice a week, it is worth investing in a rice cooker, as this will make things so much easier for you.

NOODLE BOWL (DONBURI)
As Japanese people eat soup noodles and donburi (rice with toppings) regularly, all households have the noodle bowls. Each bowl (donburi) is about 20cm wide and 12cm deep.

CHOPSTICKS (HASHI)
Two chopsticks are used to eat food in Japan. Japanese people do not use a spoon even when they eat soup. Soup is drunk out of a cup and the vegetables, tofu, seaweed, etc, are picked up with chopsticks. Japanese chopsticks have narrow ends to pick up even a small piece of food.

COOKING CHOPSTICKS (RYORI BASHI)
These are the longer, thicker chopsticks that are used for cooking. They are made with strong bamboo and are extremely durable against the high heat. They are perfect to use when deep-frying foods.

GINGER AND DAIKON GRATER (OROSHIKI)
The very fine teeth of this Japanese grater grate fresh ginger extremely finely to give a creamy texture. The coarser part of the grater is used for grating daikon (a Japanese radish or mooli). Both grated ginger and daikon are often used as a garnish for many dishes.

PESTLE AND MORTAR (SURIBACHI)
Unlike Western pestles and mortars, the mortar (bowl) of the suribachi has a sharp grating surface inside the bowl. The stick (pestle) is made from a hard wood, which is ideal for crushing sesame seeds very finely.

JAPANESE OMELETTE PAN (TAGOYAKI PAN)
This is a small rectangular pan for domestic use. A larger square one is used in an industrial kitchen. Particular Japanese egg rolls (called Tamagoyaki) cannot be made well without this pan.

CLAY POT (DONABE)

These clay pots come in different sizes. A small one is ideal for one portion and the larger ones can be for as many as 10–12 portions. A donabe is often used for winter dishes as it keeps the food hot. It can also be used in the oven.

WOODEN SPATULA (SHAMOJI)

This is a large, flat spoon used for scooping rice. It is also used when mixing the sushi rice. It can be made from bamboo, wood or plastic.

SUSHI MAT (MAKISU)

This is essential equipment when making sushi rolls. Sushi mats are made from strips of bamboo and are extremely durable and washable in hot water.

FAN (UCHIWA)

Uchiwa is a Japanese fan. They are often used for cooling people down but are also used to fan the sushi rice when mixing in the sushi vinegar.

SUSHI BARREL (HANDAI)

This is the key to making the perfect sushi rice. The combination of handai (sushi barrel), shamoji (wooden spatula) and uchiwa (fan) is essential to be able to achieve the perfect sushi rice.

WOODEN SUSHI MOULD (OSHI ZUSHI OR HAKO ZUSHI KATA)

This rectangular wooden mould is used for making compressed sushi. Traditionally this mould is soaked in water before use to prevent sushi rice sticking. However, a new and easy way to prevent the rice from sticking (instead of soaking the mould) is to put a layer of cling film between the mould and the rice.

TEMPURA PAN (TEMPURA NABE)

This pan is useful for any dishes that are deep-fried. The pan comes with a rack (that you can rest just-cooked ingredients on) that is attached on top of the pan so that the oil drips back into the pan. The tempura pan is the Japanese version of a deep-fat fryer.

Opposite page

1. Noodle bowl
2. Chopsticks
3. Omelette pan with cooking chopsticks
4. An all-purpose knife
5. Fan
6. Sushi barrel
7. Wooden sushi mould

STORE CUPBOARD INGREDIENTS

STOCK (DASHI)
Traditionally, three types of dashi stock are used in Japanese cooking. The most commonly used dashi is made with two ingredients, namely bonito flakes (katsuobushi) and sea kelp (konbu or kombu). This type of dashi is used in many Japanese dishes. The other two types of dashi are not as commonly used and are either made with little fish similar to anchovies (niboshi) or with dried shiitake mushrooms.

STOCK POWDER (DASHI NO MOTO)
Instant dashi stock is available in powder form or liquid concentrate. It is used daily by Japanese people. Simply stir the powder or liquid into boiling water.

BONITO FLAKES (KATSUOBUSHI)
These are dried shavings or flakes of a fish called Pacific bonito. Larger, coarser flakes are used to make dashi, whilst finer shavings are used as a garnish.

SEA KELP (KONBU OR KOMBU)
A type of seaweed, sea kelp or konbu (kombu) should be thick, hard and black or very dark green. Sometimes it has a white powdery surface, which is salt, but do not rinse, just wipe with kitchen paper.

RICE (KOME)
Short- or medium-grain rice is most suitable for Japanese dishes. Any kind of rice from Japan should be the right kind. Alternatively, short-grain rice from California, Australia, Spain and Korea are available in the UK and are also suitable.

NOODLES (MEN)
Soba – brown buckwheat noodles. Different flavours such as green tea or yuzu are available.
Somen – fine white wheat flour noodles.
Udon – thick white wheat flour noodles.
Kishimen – flat white wheat flour noodles.

SOY SAUCE (SHO-YU)
Soy sauce or sho-yu is a basic ingredient used in most Japanese dishes and it is the salt agent. Kikkoman is the most well-known and popular brand. Sho-yu means Japanese soy sauce. It is much less salty than the Chinese soy sauce. To achieve the traditional Japanese flavour, Chinese soy sauce is not appropriate to use in Japanese cooking. Tamari is another type of Japanese soy sauce and is often used for dipping good-quality sushi or sashimi as its consistency is thicker and richer.

SWEETENED RICE WINE (MIRIN)
This is a sweet rice wine, used for cooking only.

RICE WINE (SAKE)

This is a dry rice wine, used for both cooking and drinking. Traditionally, sake is drunk hot with a cold dish, such as sushi and sashimi, but it can be drunk cold as well.

RICE VINEGAR (KOMEZU)

Rice vinegar is milder than most western vinegars. It is mainly used for sushi rice, salad dressings and some simmered dishes. Cider vinegar can be substituted with a little water added.

SUSHI VINEGAR (SUSHIZU)

This is a special blend of rice vinegar, sugar, salt and dashi. A bottle of ready-to-use sushi vinegar is available in liquid form or in a sachet in powdered form.

CHILLI-INFUSED SESAME OIL (LAH-YU)

This is often used for Chinese and Japanese fusion dishes such as Gyoza and Ramen Noodle.

SESAME SEEDS (GOMA)

There are two types of sesame seeds used in Japanese cooking – white and black sesame seeds. White ones are untoasted and black ones are toasted. If you are using white sesame seeds, simply toast the seeds in a dry pan until they become a golden colour, before use. Toasting enhances the flavour of the seeds.

SEAWEED (KAISO)

The most commonly used seaweed in Japan is wakame. It is usually sold in dry form and is often used in soups and salads. Cooking is not required. Wakame seaweed must be soaked in water for a few minutes before using for a salad, but there is no need to soak it in water when using for a soup. The quantity/volume will increase by about ten times after soaking. Another well-known seaweed is hijiki. You must soak hijiki in water for 30 minutes first, then cooking is required afterwards.

TOASTED SEAWEED (YAKINORI OR NORI)

This is used for rolled sushi or wrapped around rice balls (onigiri). It is available as small paper-like sheets or shredded for use as sprinkles (see next entry). It should be kept in an airtight container in a cool, dry place.

DRIED SEAWEED SPRINKLES (AO-NORI)

This is a condiment for sprinkling. It has a strong flavour of seaweed and is a bright green colour.

JAPANESE MAYONNAISE (MAYONAISU)

Japanese mayonnaise is much more yellow in colour than the typical Western mayonnaise. As the colour shows, Japanese mayonnaise contains more egg yolks. It is also creamier and has a more citrusy flavour.

Opposite page

1. Yuzu concentrate
2. Chilli-infused sesame oil
3. Rice vinegar
4. (L-to-R) Soy sauce, sweetened rice wine, sushi vinegar
5. Bonito flakes
6. Stock powder
7. Rice wine
8. Toasted seaweed
9 (L-to-R) Black sesame seeds, white and toasted sesame seeds, dried wakame seaweed

1

2

3

4

5

6

7

8

9

FRESH INGREDIENTS

VEGETABLES

MOOLI (DAIKON)
Mooli or daikon is a long white radish. It is one of the most versatile vegetables and can be used for soups, salads and pickles. It is widely known as a sashimi garnish (shredded) and tempura condiment (grated).

CHINESE CABBAGE (HAKUSAI)
As the name suggests, this cabbage was originally introduced into Japan from China. In recent years, this has become one of the most popular leafy vegetables in Japanese cooking, as it is very versatile. Chinese cabbage is often used for pot dishes or it is lightly pickled to serve as a condiment.

SPINACH (HORENSO)
Japanese spinach is much firmer than the typical variety found in the UK, with reddish-coloured stems closer to the roots. It is normally displayed in a bunch with the roots attached in the shops and supermarkets. The stems are highly nutritious and packed with flavour.

SPRING ONIONS (NEGI)
There are two types of spring onions in Japan. One is very long and thick, like the Western leek. The other one is thinner, but not as small and fine as spring onions in the West. This is used for many dishes either as a garnish or just to add flavour.

JAPANESE PUMPKIN (KABOCHA)
A deep green, ragged-skinned pumpkin that is much smaller than the Western pumpkin. The flesh is very dense and deep orange in colour and is a good source of nutrients. This is traditionally used in side dishes (simmered in broth) and for tempura. In more recent years, Japanese pumpkin is often used for soups and desserts (combined with other non-Japanese ingredients such as butter and cream, making the desserts very calorific).

SWEET POTATO (SATSUMAIMO)
This is a long-shaped sweet potato with a light, burgundy-coloured skin. The flesh is pale yellow and the texture is somewhere between pumpkin and potato. It is more glutinous than potato. 'Satsuma' is the old name for the southern region of Japan. 'Imo' means potato.

YOUNG SOYA BEANS (EDAMAME)
Normally consisting of two or three beans in a hairy pod, edamame are cooked whole in boiling, salted water. As the summer is the best season for edamame, often people eat them accompanied with cold beer - it is regarded as a perfect match. In Japan, you can purchase the fresh ones, but outside of Japan, normally you will only find them frozen (in their pods).

YUZU (JAPANESE LIME)
Yuzu (or Japanese lime) is regarded as a precious citrus fruit for Japanese cooking. The rarity makes Yuzu even more popular as it is a seasonal citrus fruit. It can be used to flavour sorbets and it is also used in bath products as it is considered to be good for the skin and has a beautiful fresh scent. Fresh yuzu is difficult to get hold of outside of Japan, but concentrated yuzu juice is available in bottles.

MOUNTAIN PRODUCTS

SHIITAKE
The most well-known type of mushroom amongst Japanese mushrooms. Dark brown, with a velvety cap of about 5cm in diameter and short stalks. Shiitake mushrooms are available in both fresh and dried forms and both are widely used in Japanese cooking.

ENOKITAKE
These are interesting shaped mushrooms that have become very popular in the West in recent years. Enokitake have tiny ivory-coloured caps with very thin stalks and a crunchy texture. They are used more for their texture rather than their very subtle flavour.

SHIMEJITAKE
This is another popular Japanese mushroom. It grows in bunches and has small, light brownish-grey caps and fat stalks. The flavour is quite subtle but their unique appearance and the firm texture makes them a popular choice.

TAKENOKO
Takenoko or bamboo shoot is one of the classic ingredients of East Asia. The uniqueness of the crisp texture makes this mountain vegetable special, although it contains very few nutrients. The crispness increases dramatically if it's fresh and in season.

SOYA BEAN PRODUCTS

MISO
This is fermented soya bean paste. There are many types of miso and it is commonly used for soup but also for marinades, sauces and salad dressings. Generally, the darker in colour the miso paste is, the saltier it will be. Varieties include the normal toffee-coloured miso (most commonly used for making soup), red miso and white miso. Miso paste can be kept in an airtight container in the refrigerator for up to about 1 year, but it does get saltier as it gets older.

TOFU
Tofu is fresh bean curd and it is one of the staple foods in the Japanese diet as it is highly nutritious and low in fat. Tofu is an ivory-coloured soya bean product with a firm custard texture, available either as fresh or vacuum-packed. Silken tofu or kinu has a more delicate and soft texture than cotton tofu or momen, which has a firm, rough texture. Silken tofu tends to be used for soup and eaten as fresh, whereas the cotton tofu is used for simmered recipes and for frying. In recipes, we refer to silken tofu or firm tofu (which is the cotton tofu).

ABURAAGE (DEEP-FRIED TOFU SHEETS)
This is a golden-coloured, deep-fried bean curd. Japanese deep-fried tofu comes as rectangular, flat sheets, each sheet weighing about 20g. There are many different uses for this versatile product, such as for soups, simmered dishes, sushi, etc. As the inside is hollow and the aburaage has a durable texture, this makes it ideal for stuffing with things such as minced meat, egg, rice and so on.

HERBS AND SPICES

SHISO
This is the most popular herb for Japanese cooking. The shape of the leaf looks like nettles and the flavour is very distinctive. Shiso is a Japanese version of coriander or basil. It is often used as a garnish for the sashimi and other fresh dishes. Shiso-flavoured ready-made salad dressing is also available.

SHICHIMI TOGARASHI (SEVEN-SPICE CHILLI POWDER)
This is a combination of seven different dried and powdered spices including chilli (chilli is the predominant flavour of this spice mix). It is often served with noodle soup and fresh pickles.

SANSHO (SANSHO PEPPER POWDER)
This is dried and powdered Japanese green pepper, which is often served with teriyaki sauce in recipes such as grilled eel or teriyaki chicken.

SHOGA (GINGER)
Shoga or fresh root ginger is the most commonly used spice in Japan and it is also used in many other cuisines worldwide. Shoga is considered to be a healthy product as well as being a great flavouring for many dishes. As ginger is known to help digestion, it's often used with oily fish and meat to help break down the fat. Shoga can be served freshly grated or thinly sliced, and raw or cooked, in many dishes. The most popular way to eat ginger in the West is as pickled ginger accompanied by sushi.

WASABI (JAPANESE HORSERADISH)
Wasabi is Japanese horseradish and it is pistachio green in colour. In Japan, it is available fresh (and also in powder or paste form), but in the West it is only available as a powder or as a paste in a tube, both ready-to-use. Wasabi is often used as a garnish for sushi and sashimi and it is also used for salad dressings and cold sauces. It is very strong, just like English horseradish.

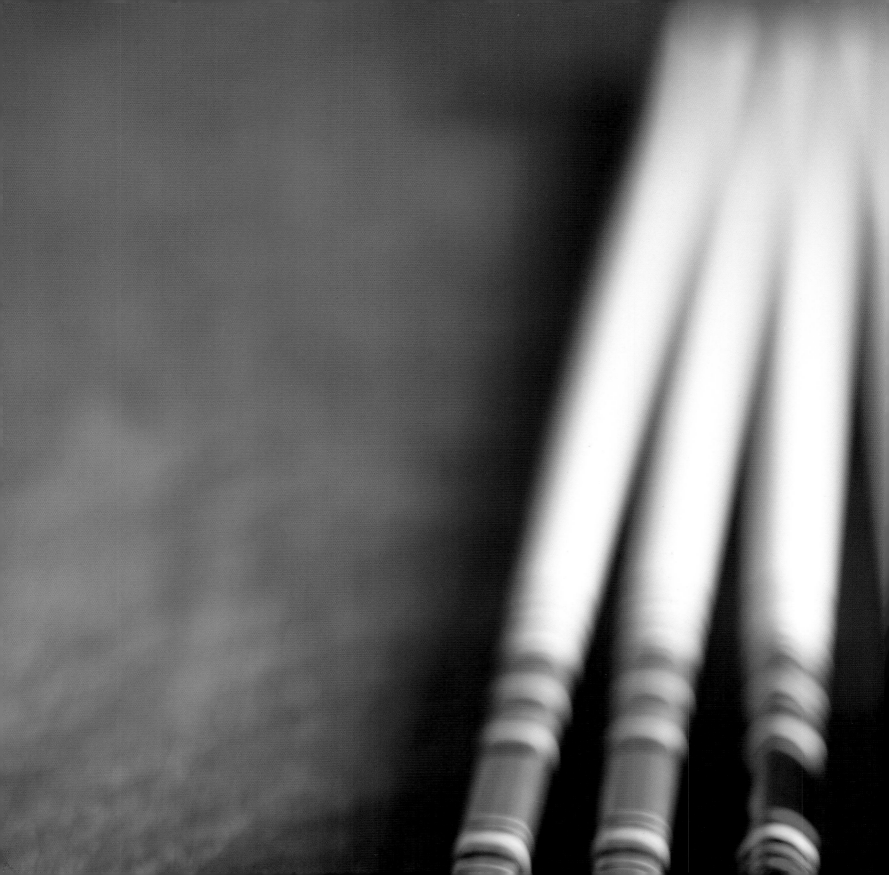

BASICS

DASHI STOCK (USING SEA KELP AND BONITO FLAKES)

20g dried sea kelp (konbu or
   kombu)
1.2 litres cold water, plus 55ml cold
   water
20g bonito flakes

MAKES ABOUT 1.1 LITRES

Place the sea kelp in a bowl, pour over 1.2 litres cold water and leave to soak for between 2–5 hours. Transfer the soaked sea kelp and soaking water to a pan and bring to the boil. Just before the mixture begins to boil, remove the sea kelp using a slotted spoon and discard (see Cook's Tip). Boil the liquid for 1 minute.

Add the bonito flakes to the pan and bring back to the boil, removing the pan from the heat just before the mixture comes to the boil. Stir in the additional 55ml cold water to cool the mixture down a little.

Allow the bonito flakes to settle on the bottom of pan, then strain the dashi stock through a muslin-lined (or kitchen paper-lined) sieve or fine mesh colander (you must not squeeze the muslin or paper to get out as much liquid as possible – just let it drip!).

Use the dashi stock as required. Store the cooled dashi stock in an airtight container in the fridge for up to 3 days or in the freezer for up to 3 months.

COOK'S TIP
You can reuse the used sea kelp and bonito flakes to make secondary dashi stock for miso soup. Alternatively, used sea kelp can be cooked to make a perfect condiment to eat with cooked rice.

DASHI STOCK (USING INSTANT DASHI POWDER)

1.2 litres cold water
2½ teaspoons instant dashi powder

MAKES ABOUT 1.2 LITRES

Bring the water to the boil in a saucepan. Add the dashi powder and stir until it is completely dissolved.

Use the dashi stock as required. Store the cooled dashi stock in an airtight container in the fridge for up to 3 days or in the freezer for up to 3 months.

VEGETARIAN STOCK

15g dried sea kelp (konbu or
   kombu)
15g dried shiitake mushrooms
1.2 litres cold water

MAKES ABOUT 1.1 LITRES

Place the sea kelp and shiitake
mushrooms in separate bowls.
Add 600ml cold water to each bowl and
leave to soak for between 2–5 hours.

Transfer the soaked sea kelp and
soaking water to a pan and bring to the
boil. Just before the mixture begins to
boil, remove the sea kelp using a slotted
spoon and discard. Boil the liquid for
1 minute, then remove from the heat
and pour the liquid into a suitable
container. Set aside.

Repeat the same procedure with the
soaked mushrooms and their soaking
liquid in the same pan.

Combine the sea kelp liquid and the
mushroom liquid in a pan, bring to the
boil and boil for 1 minute. Remove from
the heat and allow the mixture to cool
slightly. If the liquid contains small bits
from the mushrooms, strain the stock
through a muslin-lined (or kitchen-
paper lined) sieve or fine mesh colander.
Discard any bits from the sieve.

Use the stock as required. Store the
cooled stock in an airtight container
in the fridge for up to 3 days or in the
freezer for up to 3 months.

RAMEN STOCK

2 litres cold water
1 large piece fresh root ginger (about
   10cm long), peeled and roughly
   chopped
1 bunch spring onions, white parts only
300g raw chicken bones
1 large onion, quartered
4 garlic cloves, bruised
hard core of 1 white or green cabbage
   (the part normally discarded)
1 carrot, cut into chunks
220ml sake

MAKES ABOUT 1.5 LITRES

Bring the water to the boil in a large
saucepan. Add all the remaining
ingredients to the pan and bring back to
the boil, then reduce the heat, cover the
pan with a lid (but leave a small gap to
allow a little steam to escape) and
simmer gently for 2–2½ hours,
skimming the mixture from time to
time. Add a little extra water if the
liquid reduces too much during
cooking.

Strain the stock mixture through a
fine mesh colander lined with muslin.
It's best to let it strain naturally which
will take about an hour (alternatively,
you can squeeze the muslin very gently
and occasionally as the stock is being
strained). When most of the ingredients
in the colander become quite dry,
discard them.

Use the stock as required. Store the
cooled stock in an airtight container
in the fridge for up to 3 days or in the
freezer for up to 3 months.

PLAIN RICE

480g short-grain white rice
about 715ml cold water

**MAKES ABOUT 950G
COOKED RICE**

Place the rice in a sieve and wash it thoroughly using cold water until the water runs almost clear, allowing the rice to drain before rinsing again. When you first rinse the rice, the water looks like coconut milk which is the starch coming out of the rice. You need to get rid of as much starch as possible. Repeat the rinsing and draining process at least 3–4 times until the water becomes almost clear.

Place the drained rice and measured cold water (you need roughly 10% more water than the volume/quantity of rice) in a heavy-based saucepan (choose the size of the pan assuming that the rice will increase by about three times its original volume). Leave the rice to soak in the cold water for at least 30 minutes.

Place the pan containing the soaked rice over a high heat. Cover the pan with a lid (ideally the lid has a tiny hole on the top or the side to release a little steam; if not, wrap the lid with a towel, which will absorb most of the steam) and bring the mixture to the boil. Once

boiling, reduce the heat to the lowest setting and simmer for about 13–17 minutes or until all the water is absorbed (the timing for this depends on several things, for example, the quantity of rice you are cooking, what kind of pan you are using, which type of short-grain rice you are using and so on). You must keep the lid closed at all times as the steaming process is very important. If you keep opening the lid to check, you are releasing an important amount of steam every time – so you need to be very patient!

Remove the pan from the heat and allow the rice to stand and steam for a further 15 minutes with the lid tightly closed. If you are using an electric hob, you must move the pan off the hob, otherwise the rice will cook further.

COOK'S TIP
If you cook rice frequently, I strongly recommend that you purchase a rice cooker. This will make your life a hundred times easier!

SUSHI RICE

Cooked sushi rice is always served at room temperature (unless specified otherwise in a recipe).

MAKES ABOUT 600–700G COOKED SUSHI RICE

FOR THE SUSHI RICE

320g short-grain white rice
550ml cold water

FOR THE SUSHI VINEGAR

110ml rice vinegar
60g caster sugar
½ teaspoon salt
½ teaspoon concentrated dashi stock
  or instant dashi powder

NECESSARY UTENSILS

a large, flat wooden bowl/barrel
  (handai)
a large, flat wooden spatula
  (shamoji)
a fan (uchiwa)

To prepare and cook the sushi rice, follow the instructions given on page 34 for cooking plain rice.

Meanwhile, put all the ingredients for the sushi vinegar in a saucepan and heat gently, stirring occasionally. Remove the pan from the heat and set aside to cool.

Wet the inside of the wooden bowl and the wooden spatula with cold water (this will help to prevent the rice from sticking to the utensils) – see also Cook's Tip.

Transfer the steaming hot cooked rice to the wooden bowl and spread it evenly in the bowl. Gradually pour in the sushi vinegar, folding the mixture with the wooden spatula as if you are cutting through the lumps of rice and separating the grains at a sharp angle. You must fold not stir the rice, otherwise the rice grains will become crushed and lumpy.

Continue folding the rice gently, while fanning the rice using your other hand (another person's help here is very handy!) until the rice is at room temperature. Fanning is very important as it is the most efficient way to cool the temperature of the rice quickly. Once ready, the rice should be shiny and sticky but still with separate grains. Cover the rice with a piece of damp muslin cloth until you are ready to use it. This will stop the rice from drying out and becoming hardened.

COOK'S TIP
You must not use a stainless steel bowl nor a ceramic bowl because they will retain the heat from the hot rice and the condensation will make the texture of the rice too wet and gluey.

JAPANESE PICKLED VEGETABLES

SERVES 4

½ cucumber
½ Chinese cabbage or white cabbage
1 small carrot
420ml cold water
2 tablespoons salt (for rubbing on the vegetables), plus 1 teaspoon salt
5g dried wakame seaweed
a pinch of dried chilli flakes
2 teaspoons instant dashi powder

Cut the cucumber and cabbage into small bite-size pieces and slice the carrot into short, thin strips. Mix all the vegetables together in a bowl and add 200ml of the water and 2 tablespoons salt.

Rub and squeeze all the ingredients in the bowl together for about 5 minutes or until the vegetables become a little tender but are still crunchy.

Drain the water from the vegetables, then rinse the vegetables thoroughly and squeeze all the water out completely.

Place the vegetable mixture, wakame, chilli flakes, dashi powder, remaining 1 teaspoon salt and remaining 220ml water in a bowl and mix together well. Cover and chill the pickled vegetable mixture for at least 2 hours before serving.

Store in an airtight container in the fridge for up to 3 days. Drain lightly before serving and serve with soy sauce on the side.

SHO-YU DRESSING

MAKES ABOUT 100ML

2 tablespoons soy sauce
2 tablespoons vegetable oil (such as sunflower, corn or grape seed oil)
2 tablespoons rice vinegar
2 teaspoons caster sugar

Combine all the ingredients in a bowl, mixing well. Use as required.

COOK'S TIP
You can create different flavoured dressings by adding fresh flavours to the basic sho-yu dressing, as follows:

For *Wasabi Dressing*, add ½ teaspoon wasabi paste;

For *Sesame Dressing*, add 1 tablespoon ground sesame seeds;

For *Ginger Dressing*, add 1 teaspoon grated (peeled) fresh root ginger;

For *Miso Dressing*, add 1 teaspoon normal miso paste.

TERIYAKI SAUCE

200ml soy sauce
100ml sake
100ml mirin
3–4 tablespoons caster sugar

MAKES ABOUT 250ML

Put all the ingredients in a saucepan and bring to the boil. Reduce the heat and simmer, uncovered, for about 20–30 minutes or until the consistency becomes like double cream.

Use hot, warm or cold, as required (if using cold, once cool, store in the fridge until required).

PONZU SAUCE

2 tablespoons lime, lemon or yuzu
   (Japanese lime) juice
½ tablespoon rice vinegar
½ tablespoon mirin
3 tablespoons soy sauce
1 teaspoon caster sugar
½ teaspoon instant dashi powder

MAKES ABOUT 100ML

Combine all the ingredients in a bowl, mixing well. Use as required.

Put all the ingredients in a saucepan and bring to the boil. Reduce the heat and simmer, uncovered, for about 20–30 minutes or until the consistency becomes like double cream.

Use hot, warm or cold, as required (if using cold, once cool, store in the fridge until required).

DENGAKU MISO

2 tablespoons normal miso paste
2 teaspoons caster sugar
1½ tablespoons mirin

MAKES ABOUT
4 TABLESPOONS

Put all the ingredients in a small saucepan and heat gently until the ingredients are well combined, stirring occasionally – there is no need to heat or cook the mixture for very long. Alternatively, you can heat the mixture in a microwave oven on high for about 1 minute.

Use hot, warm or cold, as required (if using cold, once cool, store in the fridge until required).

GOMADARE (SESAME SAUCE)

3 tablespoons tahini paste
3 tablespoons soy sauce
1 tablespoon mirin
2 teaspoons caster sugar
1 tablespoon rice vinegar

MAKES ABOUT 100ML

Combine all the ingredients in a bowl, mixing well. Use as required.

TONKATSU SAUCE

Ready-made tonkatsu sauce can be substituted with this easy and tasty homemade version.

3 tablespoons Worcestershire sauce
2 tablespoons soy sauce
2 tablespoons caster sugar
5 tablespoons tomato ketchup
1 tablespoon sake
½–1 teaspoon English mustard

MAKES ABOUT 180ML

Put all the ingredients, except the mustard, in a small saucepan. Bring to the boil, then reduce the heat and simmer, uncovered, for about 7 minutes or until the mixture is thickened to the consistency of tomato ketchup.

Remove from the heat and cool, then stir in the mustard to taste. Use as required.

CRÈME PATISSIÈRE

6 egg yolks
120g caster sugar
30g cornflour
10g plain flour
560ml milk
1 vanilla pod, split lengthways
15g butter

MAKES ABOUT 500G

Whisk the egg yolks, sugar, cornflour and flour together in a bowl.

Put the milk and vanilla pod in a saucepan. Bring gently to the boil, then strain over the egg mixture, stirring constantly. Pour the mixture back into the saucepan and bring gently to the boil, stirring constantly. The mixture may become lumpy but if you keep stirring or whisking constantly, it will become smooth.

Continue to cook gently for a further 2 minutes, then remove from the heat and stir in the butter.

Pour the mixture into a bowl and leave to cool, whisking occasionally as it cools. Once cool, cover with cling film to prevent a skin forming. Store in the fridge for up to 2 days.

SWEET PASTRY

120g unsalted butter, at room
   temperature, diced
75g icing sugar, sifted
2 egg yolks
1 tablespoon double cream
250g plain flour
2 tablespoons cold water

MAKES ONE 24CM BAKED PASTRY CASE

Cream the softened butter and icing sugar together in a bowl. Beat in 1 egg yolk and the double cream, mixing well. Add the flour and rub the butter mixture and flour together with your fingertips to achieve a crumbly texture. Add the water and gently knead the mixture together to form a ball of dough.

Knead the dough on a lightly floured surface using the palm of your hands. Be careful not to overwork the dough or it will become hard. Flatten the dough slightly, wrap in cling film and chill in the fridge for 30 minutes.

Roll out the chilled pastry on a lightly floured surface to form a round about 3mm thick. Use the pastry to line a 24cm loose-bottomed tart tin, cutting off the excess pastry. Alternatively, you can use the pastry to line several smaller tartlet tins by cutting out smaller discs and lining each tin. Prick the base of the pastry all over with a fork and chill for a further 30 minutes. Preheat the oven to 170°C/fan 150°C/Gas Mark 3.

Line the pastry case with a sheet of greaseproof paper and fill with baking beans or raw rice. Bake in the oven for 10 minutes, then remove the baking beans and paper and bake for a further 20 minutes (smaller tartlet cases will need less cooking time). Remove from the oven and brush the inside of the pastry case with the remaining beaten egg yolk, then return to the oven for a further 1 minute to seal it. Remove from the oven and use as required..

AZUKI BEAN PASTE

120g dried azuki beans
5–6 times more cold water than the
   quantity of azuki beans
150g caster sugar
½ teaspoon salt

MAKES ABOUT 20

Put the azuki beans in a large bowl, cover with plenty of cold water and leave to soak overnight. Drain the beans, discarding the soaking water, then rinse the beans well and drain again.

Place the beans in a large saucepan with 5–6 times more cold water than the quantity of beans. Bring to the boil and boil for 1 minute, then reduce the heat to a simmer, cover and cook for about 1½–2 hours or until the beans become soft, skimming from time to time. Add some more water if necessary to keep the beans covered in water all the time. (If you have a pressure cooker, you can cook the beans in a pressure cooker and this will only take about 20 minutes.)

Add half of the sugar and the salt and cook for 2 minutes, then add the rest of the sugar and cook, uncovered, for a further 45 minutes, stirring occasionally. Turn off the heat when all the liquid has evaporated and the mixture becomes more like a paste (rather than beans cooking in liquid). Leave the mixture to cool, then store in an airtight container in the fridge for up to 1 week. This bean paste also freezes well for up to 3 months.

COOK'S TIP
Alternatively, instead of making your own, you can purchase canned cooked red bean paste from Japanese shops or some Asian supermarkets.

BEGINNERS

MISO SOUP WITH LEEK, POTATO AND DEEP-FRIED TOFU

880ml dashi stock (see recipe on page 32) or 880ml water, combined with 2 teaspoons instant dashi powder
½ leek, washed and thinly sliced
1 large potato, cut into 1cm sticks
2 sheets of deep-fried tofu, about 20g each
2 tablespoons normal miso paste
seven-spice chilli powder, to taste

This is a simple miso soup. Using potatoes and tofu make the soup quite substantial and hearty. This soup is very tasty even the next day – in fact, the flavour deepens after it has been reheated.

SERVES 4

Heat the dashi stock in a saucepan. Once the stock comes to the boil, add the leek and potato sticks and simmer for 5–6 minutes or until the potatoes are cooked and soft.

Place the deep-fried tofu in a shallow dish and pour over some boiling water to remove the excess oil. Drain the tofu well and squeeze it gently to remove the water, then cut it into 1cm slices. Set aside.

Scoop out the miso paste from the jar and add it to the soup by melting it gradually inside a ladle held in the simmering soup. This way it is easier to dissolve the miso paste evenly rather than adding the lump of miso paste all at once.

Add the sliced tofu to the soup and simmer for a further 2 minutes. Serve in individual bowls with seven-spice chilli powder served on the side.

SUMASHI-JIRU (CLEAR SOUP) WITH JULIENNE VEGETABLES

50g carrots
50g celery
50g asparagus
50g fresh shiitake mushrooms
1 sheet of deep-fried tofu (about 20g)
880ml dashi stock (see recipe on page 32)
2 tablespoons sake
2 tablespoons mirin
1½ tablespoons soy sauce
½ teaspoon salt
1 tablespoon cornflour mixed with 55ml cold water
1 tablespoon grated (peeled) fresh root ginger
seven-spice chilli powder, to taste

This is a very healthy soup. It is important to make the fresh stock for this soup since you don't add much other flavour. The key for this soup is the fresh ingredients and the fresh stock.

SERVES 4

Cut the carrots, celery and asparagus into julienne strips or thin matchsticks. Slice the mushrooms and deep-fried tofu as thinly as possible.

Put the dashi stock in a saucepan and bring to the boil, then add all the prepared vegetables and deep-fried tofu and cook for 1 minute. Add the sake, mirin, soy sauce and salt and cook for a further 2 minutes.

Gradually add the cornflour mixture to the simmering soup, stirring constantly, then bring back to the boil. The consistency of the soup should not be too thick – it should be slightly thicker than water.

Stir in the grated ginger and serve immediately with seven-spice chilli powder sprinkled over each serving.

SALMON CARPACCIO

FOR THE SALMON

110ml vegetable oil, for deep-frying
10 shallots, thinly sliced
1 ripe avocado
1 teaspoon wasabi paste
1 tablespoon soured cream
a pinch of salt
200g sashimi-quality fresh salmon
   (skinless and boneless)
2 tablespoons finely snipped fresh
   chives

FOR THE JAPANESE VINAIGRETTE

3 tablespoons vegetable oil
3 tablespoons soy sauce
3 tablespoons rice vinegar
1 tablespoon sesame oil
2 tablespoons grated onion

This is a new way of eating sashimi. It takes no time to prepare and looks beautiful. This recipe creates a great appetizer for a dinner party.

SERVES 4

Mix all the ingredients for the vinaigrette together in a small bowl. It's better to make the vinaigrette beforehand and let it sit for at least 30 minutes in the fridge so that the flavours develop well.

Prepare the salmon. Heat the vegetable oil in a small frying pan over a low heat. Add the shallots to the hot oil (not too hot or shallots will burn straight away) and deep-fry schallots slowly for about 3 minutes, keeping them moving in the oil all the time. When the shallots start to change colour, remove them to a plate lined with kitchen paper. Be careful not to cook the shallots until the colour becomes golden, as they will continue to cook a little once they have been drained. Set aside.

Halve, stone and peel the avocado. Cut the flesh into small cubes. Put the wasabi paste, soured cream and a pinch of salt in a bowl and mix together. Add the avocado to the bowl and mix gently.

Slice the salmon widthways very thinly. Arrange the sliced fish on a serving plate. Pour the vinaigrette evenly all over the fish, top with the avocado mixture, then sprinkle the chives and deep-fried shallots evenly over the top. Serve immediately.

COOK'S TIP

You can use a variety of different coloured fish, such as fresh tuna and sea bream, if you like. Arrange the different coloured slices of fish alternately on the serving plate.

NASU DENGAKU

(AUBERGINE WITH SWEET MISO SAUCE)

2 large aubergines
4 tablespoons vegetable, corn,
  sunflower or grape seed oil
6 tablespoons dengaku miso
  (see recipe on page 37)
2 teaspoons sesame seeds

You will find this dish in most authentic Japanese restaurants, hence it is a well known dish. It is an unexpectedly rich and delicious dish, so people remember it, thinking it has to be complicated to make, but in fact it's very easy to make with just a few simple ingredients.

SERVES 4

Preheat the grill to medium. Cut each aubergine in half lengthways. Brush the cut sides of each aubergine half with plenty of oil. Place under the grill and grill them for about 7 minutes, then turn them over, brush the reverse with oil, and grill for a further 7 minutes. Check the aubergines by pressing them in the middle with your finger – they should be soft like the feel of raw meat. If they still feel firm in the middle, give them a few more minutes under the grill until they are ready.

When the aubergines are cooked, remove them from the grill and then spread the miso over the top of each one. Be careful not to spread the miso too thickly or it will overpower the aubergines.

Return the aubergines to the grill for about 1–2 minutes or until the miso starts bubbling. Watch the aubergines at all times as the miso can burn very quickly.

Remove from the grill and sprinkle the sesame seeds down the middle on top of the aubergines. Serve with small forks and knives as aubergines can be difficult to eat with chopsticks.

PRAWN, CUCUMBER AND WAKAME SALAD

FOR THE SALAD
1 large cucumber
½ teaspoon salt
10g dried wakame seaweed
100g cooked peeled prawns
2cm piece fresh root ginger, peeled
    and thinly sliced
10g bonito flakes

FOR THE DRESSING
55ml rice vinegar
½ teaspoon instant dashi powder
1½ tablespoons soy sauce
3 teaspoons caster sugar
1 tablespoon mirin
1 teaspoon grated (peeled) fresh root
    ginger (optional)

This is probably the simplest dish in this book and yet the taste is very Japanese and the dish looks authentic. Your guests will be impressed with not much effort from you.

SERVES 4

Mix all the dressing ingredients together, except for ginger in a small saucepan and bring to the boil. Reduce the heat and simmer, stirring until the sugar dissolves. This will only be one or two minutes. Remove from the heat and leave to cool while preparing the salad.

For the salad, peel and halve the cucumber lengthways, then scrape out and discard the seeds. Thinly slice the cucumber flesh on the diagonal.

Place the cucumber in a small bowl, sprinkle with salt and mix together roughly. Leave to stand for 15 minutes, then transfer to a colander and rinse well under cold running water. Drain thoroughly and pat dry. Set aside.

Put the wakame in a small bowl, cover with cold water and leave to stand for 5–7 minutes or until the wakame softens. Drain and squeeze the water out.

Reserve a few prawns for the garnish. Combine the cucumber, wakame, sliced ginger, remaining prawns and the dressing in a bowl, mixing together gently. Divide the mixture between 4 individual serving bowls. Garnish each portion with the reserved prawns, sprinkle bonito flakes over the top and serve.

SPINACH WITH GOMADARE SESAME SAUCE

3 tablespoons sesame seeds
150ml gomadare (sesame sauce)
   (see recipe on page 38)
2–3 teaspoons cold water, if
   necessary
600g spinach leaves (or other green
   vegetables such as broccoli florets,
   green beans or asparagus spears)
a pinch of salt

This is a great accompaniment for most fish and meat dishes. The gomadare sesame sauce is perfect for any green vegetables, not just spinach. Even if you are not a green vegetable fan, this sauce will convert you to being a green vegetable eater!

SERVES 4

Toast the sesame seeds in a heated dry small frying pan, shaking the pan constantly. When the seeds are lightly browned and are beginning to pop, remove from the heat and leave them to cool in the pan. Once cool, reserve 1 tablespoon of the toasted seeds for garnish, then grind the remaining seeds using a pestle and mortar.

In a bowl, combine the ground seeds and gomadare. As ground sesame seeds make the sauce thicker, gradually add enough cold water until the consistency becomes like condensed milk. Set aside while you prepare and cook the vegetables.

For spinach, wash the spinach well. In a large, deep saucepan, bring some water to the boil with a pinch of salt. Immerse the spinach in the boiling water and blanch for just 15 seconds only. Drain well.

For broccoli, cut the broccoli into bite-size pieces. Cook the broccoli in a pan of boiling water, with a pinch of salt added, for about $1^{1}/_{2}$ minutes or until just tender. Drain well.

For green beans and asparagus, trim the green beans and asparagus spears. Cook them in a pan of boiling water, with a pinch of salt added, for about 3–4 minutes or until just tender. Drain well.

Rinse the cooked vegetables under cold running water until they are cold. Drain thoroughly and pat dry with kitchen paper. If you are using spinach, squeeze out the excess water.

Divide the vegetables between 4 individual serving bowls or place on a large serving plate and pour the sauce over. Sprinkle the remaining toasted sesame seeds over the top and serve.

JAPANESE COLESLAW

FOR THE VEGETABLE MIXTURE

200g Chinese cabbage, core removed
1 carrot
150g daikon radish
2 teaspoons salt
2–3 teaspoons black sesame seeds

FOR THE DRESSING

110ml Japanese mayonnaise
1 tablespoon rice vinegar
1 tablespoon sake
1 teaspoon Japanese mustard
  (not wasabi) or 2 teaspoons Dijon
  mustard
$\frac{1}{2}$ teaspoon sesame oil
1 tablespoon soy sauce
1 teaspoon caster sugar
salt and $\frac{1}{4}$ teaspoon white pepper, to
  season

Surprisingly delicious! This recipe is so easy and so different to an ordinary coleslaw. The sesame oil and the rice vinegar make this coleslaw very oriental. It is a perfect side dish for grilled fish or meat.

SERVES 4

For the vegetable mixture, finely shred the cabbage and put it in a large bowl. Cut the carrot and daikon into very thin matchsticks. (Alternatively, use a food processor with the right blade to create the thin matchsticks.)

Place the cabbage and daikon in a colander, sprinkle with the salt and roughly mix them together using your hands, then set aside for 5–7 minutes. Rinse under cold running water very well until all the salt has rinsed away, then squeeze out any excess moisture with your hands. Pat dry with kitchen paper.

Put all the ingredients for the dressing, except the salt and pepper, in a mixing bowl and mix until the dressing is well combined and has a smooth texture. Season to taste with salt and the white pepper.

Put the cabbage, daikon and carrot in a serving bowl and mix together. Just before serving, add the dressing and black sesame seeds to the vegetables and toss together to mix well.

TAMAGO-YAKI

(JAPANESE SWEET OMELETTE)

FOR THE OMELETTE

6 large eggs, beaten
3 tablespoons finely chopped fresh
   chives
60g smoked ham, finely chopped
1 teaspoon instant dashi powder
1 tablespoon mirin
2 teaspoon caster sugar
1 teaspoon soy sauce
a pinch of salt
a little vegetable or sunflower oil, for
   cooking

FOR THE GARNISH

¼ daikon radish
4 shiso leaves
a few drops of soy sauce, for
   sprinkling (optional)

If you are making this for sushi, a plain egg omelette is used. But if you are serving this as a side dish, adding the flavouring (and hence, some texture) makes it a more interesting dish.

SERVES 4

Mix all the omelette ingredients together (except the oil for cooking) in a large jug and stir well.

Heat an omelette pan over a medium heat. Soak kitchen paper in a little vegetable oil and carefully wipe the pan to grease it, or drizzle a little oil into the pan, tilting the pan to spread the oil evenly over the base.

Pour about 10% of the egg mixture into the pan. Tilt the pan to coat the base evenly with the egg mixture. When the egg starts to set, roll it up towards you using chopsticks or a spatula. Make sure you roll it while the surface of the egg is still wet or the layers of cooked omelettes won't stick to each other.

Keeping the rolled omelette in the pan, push it back to the furthest side from you. Grease the empty part of the pan again and pour another 10% of the egg mixture into the pan at the empty side of the pan. Lift up the first roll with chopsticks, and let the egg mixture run underneath. When it looks half set, roll the omelette around the first roll to make a single roll with several layers.

Repeat this procedure, making more omelettes to roll around the first two rolls (to make one multi-layered omelette roll), until you have used up half of the egg mixture. Move the omelette roll gently on to a bamboo sushi mat. Roll up the omelette firmly in the mat and leave it to stand, rolled up, for 5 minutes.

Repeat the whole process again to make another layered pancake roll with the remaining egg mixture. You will end up with two multi-layered omelette rolls.

For the garnish, grate the daikon and squeeze out the juice with your hand.

To serve, remove the sushi mats and cut the rolled omelettes into 2.5cm-thick slices. Serve garnished with the shiso leaves and grated daikon on the side, sprinkled with a few drops of soy sauce, if you like.

TAMAGO-YAKI:
ROLLING YOUR OMELETTE IN THE PAN

1. Pour the egg mixture into the pan and let it run underneath the roll.
2. Start to roll whilst the surface of the egg is still wet.
3. Continue to roll, using up all of the mixture.
4. The finished multi-layered omelette roll.

3

4

MISO MARINADE SALMON

3 tablespoons dengaku miso
(see recipe on page 37)
1 teaspoon grated (peeled) fresh root
ginger (optional)
4 pieces of salmon fillet (preferably
with the skin on)

Miso is a very versatile ingredient for Japanese cooking. Most people are familiar with its use in soup, but it is used for many other dishes, such as marinating fish and meat, sauces, dressings, curing meat and so on.

SERVES 4

Mix together the miso and ginger, if using, in a bowl. Microwave on high for 1 minute, or heat in a saucepan and simmer for 3 minutes. Leave to cool. Once the marinade has cooled down, place the salmon fillets in a shallow dish and pour over half of the marinade, turning the fish over to coat it completely. Cover and refrigerate for ideally 2 days, at least 1 whole day. Reserve the remaining marinade and keep this chilled also.

Take the salmon out of the fridge 1 hour before cooking.

Preheat the oven to the highest temperature (this will be around 240°C/fan 220°C/Gas Mark 9). Make sure the oven is properly preheated before cooking the salmon. (In case your oven is not powerful enough, try using the grill preheated to a medium-high heat.) The key point is to cook the fish quickly so you have a juicy and succulent piece of fish to eat. If you cook the fish slowly in the oven, it will dry out.

Remove the marinade from the salmon completely by wiping it off with kitchen paper (if you do not remove all the marinade, it will burn in the oven straightaway). Place the salmon fillets skin-side up on a baking tray.

Bake the salmon for about 13–15 minutes, checking occasionally to make sure the skins are not burning. If the skins are getting burnt, place a piece of foil loosely on top of the salmon but do not cover completely or the fish will be steamed. (If grilling the fish, grill it for about 4–5 minutes on each side, depending on the thickness of the fillets, turning the fish over halfway through cooking.)

Reheat the remaining marinade either in a microwave oven or in a saucepan, until it is warm. Serve the baked salmon fillets with the sauce on the side. Serve with steamed green beans or mangetout.

MACKEREL IN TERIYAKI SAUCE

2 tablespoons mirin
2 tablespoons soy sauce
1 tablespoon sake
1 tablespoon grated (peeled) fresh
    root ginger, plus extra for serving
4 mackerel fillets (with skin on),
    about 150g each
2 tablespoons cornflour
1 tablespoon vegetable oil

This is a very down-to-earth dish. Mackerel is an extremely popular fish in Japan, together with sardines, horse mackerel and herrings. These oily fish are tasty as well as being very nutritious. This economical dish can be prepared in very little time.

SERVES 4

Combine the mirin, soy sauce, sake and ginger in a shallow container, then add the mackerel fillets, turning them in the marinade to coat them all over. Cover and leave to marinate in the fridge for 20–30 minutes, turning the fish occasionally.

Remove the mackerel fillets from the marinade and pat them dry with kitchen paper. Reserve the marinade. Lightly dust the mackerel all over with the cornflour.

Heat the vegetable oil in a frying pan over a medium heat. Add the mackerel fillets to the pan, skin-side down, and cook for 1–2 minutes, depending on the thickness of the mackerel. Turn them over and cook for a further 1 minute.

Add the marinade to the pan and cook briefly to caramelise the sauce and the mackerel. Transfer the mackerel onto serving plates, skin-side down, and pour the sauce over. Top with a little more grated ginger, if you like.

SEA BASS AND PRAWN TEMPURA WITH PONZU SAUCE

FOR THE FISH AND PRAWNS

vegetable oil (at least 1 litre), for
    deep-frying
8 small fillets of sea bass, about
    50g each
8 shiso leaves
8 raw king or tiger prawns, peeled,
    rinsed and patted dry
1 tablespoon grated (peeled) fresh
    root ginger
150ml ponzu sauce, for dipping
    (see recipe on page 37)

FOR THE TEMPURA BATTER

220ml iced water
1 egg
120g plain flour mixed with 30g
    cornflour (or 150g tempura flour)

These look simple and elegant. As the deep-frying can be a little too oily, I'm using a citrusy ponzu sauce as a dipping sauce. Try using grated ginger instead of or as well as the lemon juice in the sauce.

SERVES 4

First prepare the tempura batter. Put the iced water in a bowl, add the egg and mix well. Put the combined flour and cornflour (or tempura flour) in a separate bowl. Add the egg and water mixture and stir until just mixed. It is important not to over mix. The batter should be slightly lumpy and not too smooth.

For the fish and prawns, heat the vegetable oil in a deep, heavy-based saucepan or a wok over a medium heat until it reaches 180°C. (To check the temperature of the oil, drop a little batter into the hot oil. If the batter stays in the bottom of the pan for more than 1 second, then the temperature is too low. If the batter jumps up splashing, then the temperature is too high. The batter should touch the bottom of the pan and then should immediately come up naturally to the top.)

Wrap each sea bass fillet with shiso leaves then dip the sea bass and prawns in the tempura batter, coating all over, then deep-fry them in the hot oil for 1–1½ minutes. While deep-frying the fish and prawns, gently separate them with bamboo cooking chopsticks if they are bunched together. Remove them from the pan and drain on kitchen paper.

Arrange the deep-fried fish and prawns on serving plates with a little grated ginger in the corner of each plate. Serve with the ponzu sauce in a small bowl.

SEA BASS AND PRAWN TEMPURA WITH PONZU SAUCE:
DEEP-FRYING THE TEMPURA PRAWNS

1. The prawns cooking in the oil. Use bamboo cooking sticks to keep the individual prawns apart from one another.
2. Deep-fry until the batter appears light and crispy.

1

2

SCALLOPS, PRAWNS AND SHIITAKE MUSHROOMS WITH GINGER

8 fresh shiitake mushrooms
16 mangetout
10cm long piece fresh root ginger, peeled
880ml dashi stock (see recipe on page 32)
2 tablespoons soy sauce
2 tablespoons mirin
salt and white pepper, to taste
1 tablespoon vegetable oil
8 fresh (shelled) scallops
8 fresh tiger prawns, peeled
2 tablespoons cornflour
2 tablespoons cold water

This dish has a very authentic Japanese flavour. The broth is subtle and this provides a perfect combination with the rich prawns and scallops.

SERVES 4

Score the top of each mushroom with a sharp knife to make a star shape. Blanch the mangetout in a pan of boiling water for 30 seconds. Drain and refresh under cold water, then drain again. Cut half of the ginger into needle-thin sticks and grate the rest. Set aside.

Heat the dashi stock in a deep saucepan and add the mushrooms, soy sauce, mirin and a pinch of salt. Bring to the boil.

While the dashi stock mixture is coming to the boil, heat the vegetable oil in a frying pan over a high heat. Once the pan is very hot, add the scallops and sear them quickly with a pinch of salt and pepper on both sides. Scallops only take a minute or so each side to cook, providing the pan is kept hot at all times.

While cooking the scallops, add the prawns to the stock pan. Quickly add the scallops to the stock and cook for 1 minute, then turn off the heat.

Arrange two scallops, two prawns, two mushrooms (the numbers are all depending on the size of the ingredients) and four mangetout in the middle of each deep serving dish (soup or dessert bowls are suitable) making sure all the ingredients are presented as if each ingredient is standing up and leaning towards each other.

Return the stock pan to a high heat and bring back to the boil. Mix the cornflour and water together in a small bowl until smooth. Once the stock is boiling, gradually pour in the cornflour mixture, stirring constantly, until the soup thickens – the consistency should be like double cream. Simmer for 1 minute. Squeeze the grated ginger juice into the soup and mix well.

Pour the thick soup over all the assembled ingredients in the bowls, dividing it evenly, then place the thin sticks of ginger on the very top of each portion to garnish.

BEEF AND VEGETABLE ROLLS

2 carrots
16 green beans or 8 asparagus spears
a pinch of salt
400g rib-eye beef (or fillet or sirloin),
   very thinly sliced
2 tablespoons cornflour
2 tablespoons vegetable oil
4 tablespoons soy sauce
2 tablespoons mirin
3 tablespoons sake
2 tablespoons caster sugar
1 tablespoon each tahini paste and
   rice vinegar, combined (optional)

It is important to obtain good quality, thinly sliced rib-eye beef for this recipe. Japanese shops usually sell thinly sliced beef (frozen), as this is the most popular way to eat beef. This is a very pretty dish with an appealing flavour for everyone.

SERVES 4

Cut the carrots to the size of the green beans (about 10cm long and 1cm wide).

Cook the carrots and green beans (or asparagus) with a pinch of salt in a pan of boiling water for about 5 minutes (or 3 minutes for asparagus), then drain, rinse under cold water, drain again and pat dry.

Lay the beef slices out flat and dust the top sides with cornflour. Place the cooked carrots and beans on top of the slices, dividing evenly, and roll up the beef slices, enclosing the vegetables. Lightly dust the beef rolls with cornflour. Secure the rolls with cocktail sticks.

Heat the vegetable oil in a frying pan over a medium heat. Add the beef rolls and cook until browned all over. Once the rolls are browned, reduce the heat to low and cook for a further 3 minutes, turning the beef rolls from time to time to cook every part evenly. Combine the soy sauce, mirin, sake and sugar in a small bowl, then pour this into the pan.

Increase the heat and bring the mixture to the boil, shaking the pan to roll the beef rolls around in the sauce so they absorb the flavour.

Remove the beef rolls from the pan and place on a chopping board. Leave them to rest for 1–2 minutes.

Continue simmering the remaining sauce in the pan until it becomes slightly thicker – this should take less than 1 minute. Remove from the heat and stir in the tahini paste and rice vinegar, if using, mixing well.

Slice the beef rolls into 1inch-thick slices. Place them on serving plates and pour over the thickened sauce.

TONKATSU

(CRUMBED PORK)

200g pointed or white cabbage
800g pork fillet or 4 slices of pork
  loin (about 200g each)
60g plain flour
salt and freshly ground black pepper,
  to taste
2 eggs
120–150g panko breadcrumbs
vegetable oil (at least 1 litre), for
  deep-frying
1 lemon, cut into 4 wedges
tonkatsu sauce (see recipe on page
  38), for dipping

Tonkatsu is one of the most popular and frequently eaten dishes in Japan. There are many tonkatsu restaurants in every city in Japan. Their menus are short and simple as they usually only serve tonkatsu, miso soup, rice and pickles. Traditionally, the accompaniment for tonkatsu is shredded crunchy cabbage and lemon wedges.

SERVES 4

Separate the layers of cabbage and wash thoroughly, then drain. Slice or shred the cabbage very thinly (as thinly as possible), then place in a bowl, cover with cling film and keep it in the fridge.

Trim the pork fillet by removing the membrane, then cut the meat into 20 small even-sized pieces (each piece will be about 40g). The pork loin is already cut into slices, so, if necessary, you just need to beat the meat gently using the back of a knife until each slice is about 2cm thick (gently beating the meat will also help to tenderise it further).

Season the flour with a little salt and pepper and put it on a plate. Put the eggs into a shallow dish and beat them lightly. Spread the breadcrumbs over a separate plate or shallow dish.

Dip the pieces or slices of pork first in the flour, covering them all over, then shake off any excess. Next, dip the floured pork into the beaten egg, covering completely, then finally dip the pork into the bread-crumbs, ensuring each piece or slice of pork is completely covered with breadcrumbs.

Heat the vegetable oil in a deep, heavy-based saucepan or a wok over a medium heat until it reaches 170°C. (To check the temperature of the oil, drop a few breadcrumbs into the hot oil. If the breadcrumbs touch the bottom of the pan and then rise up smoothly, the oil is ready. If the breadcrumbs stay on the bottom for a while, this means the oil temperature is too low.)

Slide the pork into the hot oil. Deep-fry the pork for about 2–3 minutes for the fillet pieces and 4–5 minutes for the loin slices, turning them occasionally. Once the breadcrumb coating becomes light golden brown in colour, remove the meat from the pan and drain on kitchen paper. Leave it to rest for 1 minute.

Cut the loin meat into 1cm-thick slices. Place some of the shredded cabbage onto each serving plate, then place the meat on the other side of the plates. Serve each portion with a lemon wedge on the side of the meat and serve the tonkatsu sauce separately.

GINGER PORK

2 tablespoons soy sauce
2 tablespoons sake
1 tablespoon mirin
1½ teaspoons caster sugar
1 tablespoon grated (peeled) fresh
   root ginger
600g pork loin, thinly sliced
2 tablespoons vegetable oil

The key to success with this recipe is to prepare everything in advance and cook it quickly. If you cook the pork slowly, it becomes chewy. If you crowd the pan, the pork will be boiled. Use one large frying pan to cook two portions at once. This may not be a perfect dinner party dish but it is suitable for a hearty mid-week meal, instead of curry perhaps!

SERVES 4

Mix the soy sauce, sake, mirin, sugar and ginger together in a bowl. Lay the sliced pork out evenly on a large plate and pour over half of the ginger mixture. Leave to marinate at room temperature for 15 minutes.

Heat the vegetable oil in a large frying pan over a high heat. Take the pork slices one by one and lay each one flat in the pan. Cook for 1 minute or until one side is nicely caramelised, then turn them over one by one and cook for a further 1 minute. The pork should be nicely coated with caramelised marinade.

Transfer the pork onto warm serving plates. Quickly pour the rest of the ginger mixture into the pan and cook until it is slightly thickened. Pour the sauce over the pork and serve immediately with crunchy stir-fried vegetables.

YAKITORI

(CHICKEN ON SKEWERS)

220ml teriyaki sauce (see recipe on
    page 37)
2 tablespoons cold water
600g skinless, boneless chicken thigh
    fillets, cut into 2.5cm cubes
1 large red pepper, deseeded and cut
    into 2.5cm squares
1 large green pepper, deseeded and
    cut into 2.5cm squares
seven-spice chilli powder, chilli
    powder or sansho pepper, to serve
    (optional)

12–16 bamboo skewers

Yakitori is one of the most well-known dishes next to sushi and tempura outside of Japan. It is indeed tasty, presentable and easy to eat. There are many Yakitori restaurants in Japan, which are more like pub equivalents in the West rather than restaurants. People go there to enjoy cold Japanese beer whilst they nibble on skewers of yakitori.

SERVES 4

Put 165ml of the teriyaki sauce in a bowl, add the water and mix together (reserve the remaining teriyaki sauce for serving). Put the chicken pieces in a shallow dish, pour over the teriyaki mixture, turning the chicken pieces to coat them all over. Cover and leave to marinate in the fridge overnight or for at least 5 hours. (If you only have less than 2 hours to marinate, rub the sauce into the chicken, as this will help the flavour to be absorbed more quickly.)

Preheat the oven to the highest temperature (this will be around 240°C/fan 220°C/Gas Mark 9. Cover a large baking tray with foil. Thread three pieces of chicken onto each skewer, followed by a piece of each pepper, then three pieces of chicken again, followed by a piece of each pepper. Repeat this until you have used up all the chicken and peppers (dividing the ingredients evenly between the skewers).

Lay the skewers on the prepared baking tray, then cover the bare parts of the skewers with foil (by folding the foil over the ends of the skewers or covering them with an extra piece of foil (this will prevent the skewers from burning). Cook in the oven for about 10 minutes, then turn them over and quickly brush with the teriyaki marinade sauce. Return to the oven and cook for a further 4–5 minutes or until they are thoroughly cooked. The key is to cook the chicken skewers quickly. If you cook them slowly the chicken will dry out, so make sure the oven is *very* hot. If your oven is not powerful enough, use a grill (preheated to medium-high) making sure you turn the skewers over from time to time.

Place the cooked chicken skewers in each serving dish and brush them with the reserved teriyaki sauce. Serve immediately with the seasoning of your choice, if you like.

TERIYAKI CHICKEN

220ml teriyaki sauce (see recipe on page 37)
2 tablespoons cold water
600g boneless chicken thigh fillets (with skin on)
chilli powder, sansho pepper or wasabi paste, to serve (optional)

While yakitori chicken is eaten more so in the restaurants and street fairs, teriyaki is eaten at home and it does take less time to prepare. Both recipes use the same flavours and the same part of the chicken. Teriyaki chicken uses similar ingredients to those used for yakitori chicken but no vegetables and skewers are needed. However, you might want to serve this chicken with some green vegetables or a salad from the previous recipes.

SERVES 4

Put 165ml of the teriyaki sauce in a bowl, add the water and mix together (reserve the remaining teriyaki sauce for serving). Open up each chicken thigh into flat pieces. Place the chicken thighs in a shallow dish, pour over the teriyaki mixture, turning the chicken pieces to coat them all over. Cover and leave to marinate in the fridge overnight or for at least 5 hours. (If you only have less than 2 hours to marinate, rub the sauce into the chicken, as this will help the flavour to be absorbed more quickly.)

Preheat the grill to medium-high. Lay the chicken thigh fillets, skin-side down, on the rack in a grill pan in a single layer. Grill for about 3 minutes, then turn the chicken over and reduce the temperature to medium. Grill the chicken, skin-side up, for a further 5–7 minutes or until it is thoroughly cooked. Alternatively, you can cook the chicken in a frying pan if you prefer – see Cook's Tip, right.

Place the chicken on a chopping board, skin-side up, and rest for 1 minute. Slice the chicken into 1cm-thick slices and place on a plate. Pour the reserved teriyaki sauce over the chicken and serve with a crunchy salad or crunchy green vegetables such as green beans, asparagus or broccoli. Serve the chicken with your chosen seasoning on the side, if you like.

COOK'S TIP

To cook the chicken thigh fillets in a frying pan, heat a frying pan over a medium heat, then add a little vegetable oil. Place the chicken fillets, skin-side up, in the pan and cook for about 2 minutes. Turn the chicken over, reduce the heat to medium-low and cook for about 5 minutes or until the chicken is fully cooked, covering the pan with a lid but making sure to leave a little gap for the steam to escape.

COLD SOBA NOODLE AND PRAWNS

FOR THE SOBA NOODLE SALAD

250g–300g dried soba noodle
  (buckwheat noodle)
1 tablespoon dried wakame seaweed
150g cooked peeled prawns
1 cucumber
1 tablespoon very thinly sliced
  (peeled) fresh root ginger or grated
  ginger (optional)
2 tablespoons finely chopped spring
  onions (cut on the diagonal)
1 tablespoon toasted sesame seeds

FOR THE DRESSING

4 tablespoons soy sauce
2 tablespoons mirin
2 tablespoons rice vinegar
2 teaspoons caster sugar
1 tablespoon cold water
1 teaspoon sesame oil
1 teaspoon grated (peeled) fresh
  root ginger
3 tablespoons sesame seeds, toasted
  and ground

This creates a perfect light summer lunch, or it is an ideal accompaniment for a barbecue. As it is served cold, you can treat this dish as a salad – but a substantial and satisfying salad! Soba noodle is made with buckwheat flour that gives you plenty of energy but it is low in calories.

SERVES 4

For the soba noodle salad, break the dried soba noodle in half. Cook the noodles in a large pan of boiling water, according to the packet instructions (normally for about 4–5 minutes). Drain, rinse under cold running water, then drain again thoroughly. Set aside.

Meanwhile, soak the wakame seaweed in cold water for about 5 minutes. Drain, then squeeze the water out. Cut the prawns into small bite-size pieces. Trim off both ends of the cucumber, then peel and cut in half lengthways. Scrape out and discard the seeds, then thinly slice the cucumber diagonally. Cut the sliced ginger into needle-thin sticks, if using.

In a large bowl, combine the drained noodles, wakame seaweed, prawns, cucumber and spring onions.

Combine all the dressing ingredients in a separate bowl and mix together well. Pour the dressing over the noodle mixture and toss together to mix. Sprinkle with the ginger sticks or grated ginger, if using, and the toasted sesame seeds.

SOMEN NOODLES WITH SPICY AUBERGINES

880ml dashi stock (see recipe on
   page 32)
4 tablespoons soy sauce
4 tablespoons mirin
2 tablespoons sake
1–2 teaspoons caster sugar
a pinch of salt
2 large aubergines
vegetable oil (at least 1 litre), for
   deep-frying
4 small fresh red chillies, deseeded
   and chopped
300g dried somen or soba noodles
2 tablespoons grated (peeled) fresh
   root ginger
4 tablespoons chopped spring onions
2 tablespoons sesame seeds

This is a surprisingly rich, but light and healthy noodle dish, combining simple ingredients with strong flavours, perfect as a summer dish. The key is to deep-fry the aubergines well.

SERVES 4

Put the dashi stock, soy sauce, mirin, sake, sugar and salt in a saucepan, bring to the boil, then reduce the heat and simmer for about 10–15 minutes or until all the flavours are well blended. Remove from the heat and leave it to cool. Once it's cooled down you can keep this sauce in an airtight container in the fridge for up to 1 week.

Cut the aubergines into long, thin slices (leaving the skin on). Heat the vegetable oil in a large, heavy-based saucepan or a wok over a medium heat until it reaches 170°C. (To check that the temperature of the oil is hot enough, see method of Tonkatsu recipe on page 38.)

Deep-fry the aubergines in the hot oil for about 2–3 minutes, depending on how hard they are (if the aubergines are hard, they will take longer to cook and if they are soft like a sponge, they take a much shorter time to cook). Once cooked, remove the aubergines from the pan and drain on kitchen paper. Leave them to cool. Quickly deep-fry the chopped chillies for about 30 seconds, then remove and drain on kitchen paper.

Cook the noodles in a large pan of boiling water for 2–3 minutes for somen noodles or for 4–5 minutes for soba noodles. Drain the noodles, rinse under cold running water, making sure they cool down completely, then drain thoroughly.

Stir the grated ginger into the cold sauce you made earlier. Ideally, leave it to infuse for about 5 minutes, but if you don't have time, just mix it very well.

Divide the cold noodles evenly between 4 serving plates and place the aubergines on top of the noodles. Pour the sauce over, then sprinkle the deep fried chillis, the spring onions and sesame seeds over the top. Serve immediately as the noodles soak up all the sauce very quickly.

TAKIKOMI GOHAN

(FLAVOURED RICE)

320g short-grain white rice
330ml cold water
440ml warm water
½ teaspoon caster sugar
6 small dried shiitake mushrooms
100g skinless, boneless chicken thigh
    fillets
1 carrot
1½ teaspoons instant dashi powder
3 tablespoons soy sauce
1 tablespoon mirin
1 tablespoon sake
¼ teaspoon salt, plus a pinch of salt
30g mangetout

This is a cheap and cheerful, healthy, tasty and extremely easy dish, and it only uses one pan. Why not try it? Once you cook this dish, you will find yourself cooking it on a weekly basis, I guarantee! Also try using different meat, fish or vegetables for a change.

SERVES 4

Wash the rice, place it in a pan and cover with the cold water. Leave to soak for 1–5 hours. At the same time, combine the warm water and sugar in a bowl, add the dried mushrooms and leave to soak for 1–5 hours (sugar makes the mushrooms soft and plump more quickly).

Cut the chicken into 1cm cubes and chop the carrot into thin 2cm sticks. Drain the shiitake mushrooms, reserving half of the soaking liquid. Chop off and discard the stems from the mushrooms, then slice the caps thinly.

Place all the remaining ingredients (except the pinch of salt and the mangetout), including the reserved mushroom soaking liquid, the mushrooms, chicken and carrots, on top of the soaked rice in the pan and stir gently to mix. Cover and bring to the boil, then reduce the heat and simmer for about 15 minutes or until all the liquid has been absorbed and the rice is cooked. Remove from the heat, then set aside to steam naturally, without any heat and with the lid on, for a further 15 minutes.

Meanwhile, in a separate small pan of boiling water with a pinch of salt added, blanch the mangetout for about 20 seconds. Drain, rinse under cold water and drain again. Cut the mangetout thinly on the diagonal.

Once the rice is ready, take off the lid and stir the rice gently. Serve the flavoured rice in individual rice bowls or in a large bowl for the table and sprinkle the mangetout on top. Serve immediately.

MISO ZOSUI

(JAPANESE RISOTTO)

1 litre dashi stock (see recipe on
   page 32)
240g cooked Japanese (short-grain
   white) rice (it is better to use rice
   cooked the previous day and kept
   in the fridge overnight)
2 Chinese cabbage leaves, thinly
   sliced
2 rashers streaky bacon, cut into
   thin strips
2 tablespoons normal miso paste
2 tablespoons white miso paste
3–4 tablespoons boiling water
100g frozen green peas or frozen
   edamame beans (young soya
   beans) (shelled weight)
2 spring onions, thinly sliced
4 eggs
deep-fried shallots, to garnish
seven-spice chilli powder, to taste
finely chopped (drained) Japanese
   pickled vegetables (see recipe on
   page 36), to serve

Zosui is a comfort food in many countries. Risotto in Italy, Conjee in China and Zosui in Japan... There are many ways to enjoy the zosui by using a variety of ingredients and spices. This is an ideal dish for a diet as it is both tasty and satisfying.

SERVES 4

Heat the dashi stock in a saucepan until it is boiling. Once it starts to boil, add the cooked rice, Chinese cabbage and bacon, then reduce the heat to a simmer.

Meanwhile, melt both types of miso together in a small cup with the boiling water to make a thin paste. If you don't have white miso, just one kind of miso can be used.

Simmer the rice and cabbage for 10 minutes, then add the miso paste, green peas or beans and spring onions to the pan, mixing well. Simmer for a few more minutes or until the peas/beans are cooked.

Crack the eggs into the rice. Put the lid on and continue to simmer for 2 minutes. Be careful not to overcook the eggs as the yolks are better when they are still runny.

Serve the risotto in individual bowls with one egg each. Sprinkle the deep-fried shallots on top to garnish. Serve with the seven-spice chilli powder and Japanese pickles as condiments.

AGEDASHI DOFU

(DEEP-FRIED TOFU WITH THICK BROTH)

600g silken tofu (2 cakes/blocks
    of tofu)
880ml dashi stock (see recipe on
    page 32)
4 tablespoons mirin
2 tablespoons soy sauce
½ teaspoon salt
120g cornflour, for dusting, plus
    1 tablespoon for thickening the
    stock
vegetable oil (at least 1 litre), for
    deep-frying
5cm piece fresh root ginger, peeled
    and grated
2 tablespoons chopped spring onions
bonito flakes, to garnish

**As is often the case, the simple dishes are the most complex to perfect.
With this recipe, the skill is to deep-fry the tofu so that it remains crispy
on the outside and soft and smooth inside. The key is getting the oil to
the right temperature and getting all the rest of the ingredients ready
before frying the tofu.**

SERVES 4

Drain the tofu, then wrap it in kitchen paper and place it on a chopping board with another heavy chopping board placed on top. Leave it for 1 hour so the excess moisture is pressed out.

In a saucepan, combine the dashi stock, mirin, soy sauce and salt. Bring to the boil, then reduce the heat and simmer for about 5–7 minutes.

Meanwhile, cut each tofu cake/block into 4 pieces, pat dry with kitchen paper, then coat all over with the cornflour.

Heat the vegetable oil in a deep, heavy-based saucepan or a wok over a medium heat until it reaches 180°C. (To check that the temperature of the oil is hot enough, see method of Tonkatsu recipe on page 38.)

Carefully add the tofu pieces to the hot oil, taking care not to break them. Deep-fry for about 2 minutes or until the tofu pieces turn a light golden colour. Tofu doesn't need to cook but it needs to be warmed through inside.

Remove the tofu and place on kitchen paper to remove the excess oil.

In a small bowl, combine the remaining 1 tablespoon cornflour with 2 tablespoons cold water. Increase the heat for the stock pan. Stir the blended cornflour mixture into the stock, stirring constantly, until the stock becomes slightly thicker in consistency. Simmer for 1 minute.

Put 2 pieces of deep-fried tofu into each serving bowl. Pour the stock into each bowl from the side, taking care not to wet the top of the tofu (the top half of the tofu should be left crispy), dividing the stock evenly. Garnish with the grated ginger, spring onions and bonito flakes sprinkled on top of the tofu.

MISO DOFU

(TOFU IN SWEET MISO SAUCE)

3 tablespoons sake
3 tablespoons mirin
1 teaspoon caster sugar
330ml dashi stock (see recipe on
 page 32)
3 tablespoons normal miso paste
400g firm tofu
10g bonito flakes
a handful of small watercress sprigs,
 roughly chopped
2 teaspoons wasabi paste, to serve

Miso dofu is simple and extremely comforting. It is a perfect winter dish when you don't feel like spending too much time in the kitchen. The taste varies depending on which types of miso you use, but whichever type you choose, this dish will make you smile. You can always try adding cooked plain rice or noodles to any leftover sauce and serve with a sprinkling of chopped spring onions, for a change.

SERVES 4

Put the sake, mirin and sugar into a flameproof casserole dish or a heavy-based saucepan and gently simmer for two minutes, then add the dashi stock and miso paste, stirring to make sure the miso paste is dissolved completely in the liquid with no lumps. Bring the mixture to the boil.

Meanwhile, quickly wash and drain the tofu and cut into 2.5cm cubes. Add the tofu cubes to the miso mixture in the pan, making sure all the tofu cubes are covered. Bring back to the boil, then reduce the heat and simmer for 18–20 minutes, ladling the miso sauce over the tofu cubes from time to time.

Divide the tofu between 4 individual serving bowls and pour over the thick miso sauce. Top with the bonito flakes and chopped watercress and serve with the wasabi paste on the side.

TOFU AND AVOCADO SALAD WITH WASABI DRESSING

FOR THE SALAD

400g silken tofu
1 large avocado
1 teaspoon lemon juice
80g good-quality crab sticks or
    canned crab meat
¼ onion, thinly sliced
20g fresh flat-leaf parsley, roughly
    chopped
1 teaspoon toasted sesame seeds

FOR THE WASABI DRESSING

1 teaspoon wasabi paste
1 tablespoon soy sauce
½ teaspoon salt
2 tablespoons lemon juice
3 tablespoons extra-virgin olive oil

This is a refreshing salad, ideal for the summer. Tofu, avocado and crab all go very well with the sharp flavour of wasabi. All the different textures and colours in this recipe make this an elegant and interesting dish.

SERVES 4

For the salad, drain the tofu, then wrap it in kitchen paper and place it on a chopping board with another heavy chopping board placed on top. Leave it for 1 hour so the excess moisture is pressed out, then refrigerate the tofu for at least 1 hour.

Halve, stone and peel the avocado. Cut the flesh diagonally into slices. Sprinkle the lemon juice over the avocado and gently toss, making sure all the avocado slices are coated with lemon juice.

Unwrap the crabsticks and tear them into flakes by hand. If you are using the canned crab meat, drain it and make sure there are no bones.

Mix all the dressing ingredients together in a small bowl.

Cut the tofu into large bite-size cubes and lay them in lines on a serving plate or platter. Gently toss the avocado, crab, onion and parsley together in a bowl, then place this mixture on top of the tofu. Pour the wasabi dressing over the top just before serving. Sprinkle with sesame seeds and serve.

STEAMED SCALLOPS AND TOFU WITH SESAME FLAVOUR

300g silken tofu
2 fresh shiitake mushrooms
a handful of fresh coriander leaves
160g fresh (shelled) scallops
1 large egg
salt and white pepper, to taste
1 tablespoon cornflour
a pinch of baking powder
1–2 tablespoons sesame oil
1–2 tablespoons soy sauce
3 tablespoons finely chopped spring
   onions

The richness of scallops and the subtle flavour of tofu are a perfect match, and the sesame oil and coriander give a good kick to the flavour. If you are a vegetarian, try this dish simply without the scallops.

SERVES 4

Wrap the tofu in kitchen paper or muslin cloth and squeeze out as much water as possible. Set aside.

Dust off the shiitake mushrooms with a damp cloth, cut off and discard the stalks and chop the caps finely. Roughly tear or chop the coriander leaves. Set aside.

Cut the scallops into small bite-size pieces and place in a large flat bowl. Break up the tofu with a fork in a separate bowl. Add the crushed tofu and the shiitake mushrooms to the bowl containing the scallops and mix well.

Beat the egg with 2 pinches of salt and pepper in a small bowl, then mix this into the tofu mixture. Add the cornflour and baking powder and mix together roughly.

Place the whole bowl in a large steamer, cover and steam for about 30 minutes or until just set. If you are using a microwave, cover the bowl with cling film (leaving a small gap to allow steam to escape) and cook on medium-high (about 50–60% power) for 5–7 minutes.

Meanwhile, heat the sesame oil, soy sauce and spring onions together in a small saucepan and cook for 1 minute. Pour the sauce over the cooked tofu dish and sprinkle coriander over the top to garnish. Serve.

HOME COOKS

TONJIRU

(CHUNKY ROOT VEGETABLES AND PORK MISO SOUP)

1 carrot, trimmed
5cm piece daikon radish
½ sweet potato or ¼ butternut
squash or 1 standard potato
1 courgette, trimmed
¼ leek, washed
1.2 litres dashi stock (see recipe on
page 32) or 1.2 litres cold water,
plus 2½ teaspoons instant dashi
powder
150g pork belly or skinless boneless
chicken thighs, cut into thin (5mm)
slices, or 50g unsmoked streaky
bacon, cut into thin strips
3–4 tablespoons normal miso paste
finely chopped spring onions, to
garnish (optional)
seven-spice chilli powder, to serve

**Tonjiru is a most comforting miso soup. It's hearty, healthy and filling.
If you add cooked rice or noodles, you have everything you want in one
bowl. It is a great winter dish when you don't want to fuss about cooking.**

SERVES 4

Cut all the vegetables into bite-size
pieces. Try to cut them into different-
shaped pieces to make the soup look
more interesting. Set aside.

Heat the dashi stock or water in a
medium saucepan until it is boiling.
If you are using instant dashi powder,
add the powder when the water is
boiling.

Add the pork, chicken or bacon to
the dashi stock and cook for about
3 minutes. Add the daikon radish and
cook for about 3–4 minutes, skimming
any brown scum off the surface from
time to time.

Add the rest of the vegetables and
continue to cook over a medium-low
heat for a further 5 minutes.

Scoop out about 110ml of the hot stock
into a small bowl, add the miso paste
and mix to loosen the paste in the
liquid. Add the miso mixture to the pan
and mix well.

Pour the soup into individual soup
bowls and garnish each portion with a
sprinkling of chopped spring onions,
if you like. Serve the seven-spice chilli
powder as a condiment.

CLEAR SOUP WITH MINCED CHICKEN BALLS

FOR THE CHICKEN BALLS

300g minced chicken
4 dried shiitake mushrooms, soaked
  in sugared water (see Cook's Tip),
  drained and finely chopped
1 tablespoon finely chopped spring
  onions
$^{1}/_{2}$–1 teaspoon cornflour
1 teaspoon soy sauce
$^{1}/_{2}$ teaspoon sake
$^{1}/_{2}$ teaspoon mirin
1 teaspoon grated (peeled) fresh root
  ginger
1 egg
a pinch of salt

FOR THE SOUP

1.3 litres dashi stock (see recipe on
  page 32)
2 teaspoons soy sauce
2 teaspoons mirin
a pinch of salt
50g baby spinach leaves, rinsed
2 teaspoons very thinly sliced
  (peeled) fresh root ginger

Chicken and shiitake mushrooms give a great flavour to this subtle clear soup. You may like to try adding a little fresh chilli or some fresh herbs.

SERVES 4

Combine all the ingredients for the chicken balls in a bowl and mix together well. Divide the mixture into 12–16 portions (depending on the size of balls required) and roll each portion into a ball. Set aside.

For the soup, heat the dashi stock in a saucepan with the soy sauce, mirin and a pinch of salt.

When the stock mixture starts to boil, turn the heat up to high, then drop the chicken balls one by one into the stock using two teaspoons. When you have finished adding the chicken balls, reduce the heat to medium-low and simmer for about 5 minutes. Skim the surface occasionally, if necessary, while simmering.

When the chicken balls start coming up to the surface of the soup and float, add the spinach leaves and cook for 20 seconds.

Divide the soup between 4 individual bowls and sprinkle each portion with some sliced fresh ginger.

COOK'S TIP
When you hydrate dried mushrooms in water, add a little sugar to the soaking water as this will help the mushrooms to plump up more quickly. The ratio for the sugared water should be about $^{1}/_{4}$–$^{1}/_{2}$ teaspoon caster sugar to 220ml warm water.

GYOZA

(SHALLOW-FRIED AND STEAMED DUMPLING)

FOR THE FILLING

150g fresh peeled prawns or
  prepared fresh squid, washed
  and patted dry
200g minced pork or chicken
½ pointed cabbage, finely chopped
1 bunch spring onions, finely
  chopped
a handful of fresh coriander leaves
2 garlic cloves, grated
1 tablespoon soy sauce
½ teaspoon white pepper
1 tablespoon mirin
1 tablespoon sake
1 teaspoon sesame oil
1–2 teaspoons cornflour
50–60 gyoza dumpling wrappers
  (see Cook's Tip)
2 tablespoons vegetable oil
110ml cold water

FOR THE DIPPING SAUCE

2 tablespoons soy sauce
2 tablespoons rice vinegar
1 tablespoon mirin
1 tablespoon sesame oil
½ teaspoon dried chilli flakes
  or chilli paste (optional)

The key to success with Gyoza is to cook it properly. You cook this dish in a frying pan with a lid, so that the bottom becomes crispy but the whole dumpling is steamed and juicy. It is very easy and economical to make. All you need is a little bit of time and patience to make many pretty dumplings – it's well worth it!

SERVES 4

Mix all the dipping sauce ingredients together in a small bowl and set aside.

For the filling, finely chop and grind the seafood until it becomes creamy in texture. Mix all the filling ingredients, except the gyoza wrappers, vegetable oil and cold water, together in a large bowl using your hands. The consistency should be firm enough to form a ball but not too dry. If you feel the filling is too wet, then add a little more cornflour.

Place a gyoza wrapper in your flat left hand (or your non-leading hand) and wet two-thirds of the edge with water. Place a teaspoonful of filling in the centre of the wrapper and fold over the wrapper. Make creases on the wet side of the wrapper, then pinch and stick the edges together to seal and make a small parcel or dumpling. Repeat with the rest of the filling and wrappers until you have used them all up.

Heat the vegetable oil in a large frying pan over a medium-high heat, then place the dumplings in four lines in the pan. Pour the water into the pan and cover the pan with the lid, leaving a small gap to allow some steam to escape. Cook over a medium heat for 5 minutes or until all the water has evaporated. Take the lid off, turn the heat up to high and cook for a further 1 minute or until the bottom of the dumplings are browned and crispy.

To serve, use a palette knife to scoop out one line of dumplings and quickly place them on a serving plate, turning them over so that the crispy sides will show. Repeat for the remaining portions. Serve immediately with the dipping sauce on the side.

COOK'S TIPS
You can buy the gyoza dumpling wrappers either in Japanese shops or in any Asian supermarket. They are normally sold frozen, so defrost them slowly in the fridge before use.
For the dipping sauce, if you can get hold of lah-yu (chilli-infused sesame oil), use this instead of the sesame oil and chilli listed.

BROCCOLI WITH MISO AND SESAME SAUCE

200g broccoli
1 teaspoon salt
2 tablespoons black sesame seeds
2 tablespoons white or normal miso paste
1 teaspoon caster sugar
1 tablespoon mirin
1 tablespoon soy sauce
1 teaspoon rice vinegar
1 teaspoon tahini paste (optional)

With this dish, just a humble vegetable such as broccoli can be made into something so interesting and delicious. The florets absorb the miso and sesame sauce and this becomes not only a great vegetable side dish but it also stamps its own mark on a meal.

SERVES 4

Trim the broccoli into large bite-size pieces and wash them thoroughly. Add the salt to a large pan of water and bring to the boil (the salt will help to retain the bright green colour of the broccoli). Cook the broccoli in the boiling water for 2 minutes. Drain, rinse under cold water, drain again and leave the broccoli in a colander to dry.

Lightly crush the sesame seeds using a pestle and mortar. Set aside.

Combine the miso paste, sugar, mirin, soy sauce and vinegar in a small bowl and mix them together to make a smooth paste. You can stir in the tahini paste if you like (tahini makes the mixture slightly richer and creamier).

Put the broccoli into a large mixing bowl, add the miso sauce and crushed sesame seeds and toss together until the broccoli is well coated. Serve.

COOK'S TIPS
You can also use white sesame seeds instead of black ones, if you prefer. White miso paste is sweeter. You can mix normal and white miso pastes together, if you prefer. Also, green beans make a great substitute for broccoli in this recipe.

HIJIKI SEAWEED WITH DEEP-FRIED TOFU AND CARROTS

40g dried hijiki seaweed
2 sheets of deep-fried tofu, about
    20g each
1 tablespoon vegetable oil
1 small carrot, cut into thin
    matchsticks
100ml cold water
½ teaspoon instant dashi powder
2 tablespoons sake
2 tablespoons caster sugar
3 tablespoons soy sauce

This is almost like a condiment for a Japanese table. It's great with plain rice, but also does not overpower other dishes. Very healthy ingredients are used in this recipe. If you prefer to be extra healthy, try using less sugar!

SERVES 4

Soak the hijiki seaweed in plenty of cold water for about 30 minutes. Drain the seaweed in a colander and wash it under cold running water. Drain completely.

Bring a pan of water to the boil and blanch the deep-fried tofu in the boiling water for 1 minute. Drain, rinse under cold running water, then drain again and squeeze the tofu sheets until they are almost dry, taking care not to tear them. Cut the tofu sheets into 3 x 1cm strips.

Heat the vegetable oil in a large saucepan, add the carrot sticks and stir-fry for 2 minutes or until half cooked. Add the hijiki seaweed and stir-fry over a medium heat for a further 1 minute.

Add the water, dashi powder, sake, sugar, soy sauce and deep-fried tofu strips to the pan, then lower the heat to a simmer. Cook for about 5 minutes or until most of the cooking liquid has evaporated.

Remove the pan from the heat and leave to stand, covered, for about 10 minutes. Serve warm or cold.

KAKIAGE

(SEAFOOD AND VEGETABLE MIXED TEMPURA)

FOR THE TEMPURA

200g fresh peeled prawns or
   prepared fresh squid, washed and
   patted dry
100g deseeded yellow pepper, thinly
   sliced
½ leek, thinly sliced
100g watercress, roughly chopped
120g tempura flour (kept chilled in
   the fridge)
110ml ice-cold water
vegetable oil (at least 1 litre), for
   deep-frying

FOR THE DIPPING SAUCE

1 quantity of ponzu sauce (see recipe
   on page 37)
2 tablespoons grated daikon radish

**This is a more down-to-earth tempura. You can make small ones
(as I have done in this recipe) or one large disc, as you wish. The seafood
and the vegetable flavours mingle so well in this dish.**

SERVES 4

Mix the dipping sauce ingredients
together in a bowl and set aside.

For the tempura, cut the prepared
seafood into small pieces. In a bowl,
roughly mix the seafood, yellow pepper,
leek and watercress together with the
cold tempura flour and water.

Heat the vegetable oil in a wok over a
medium heat until it reaches 170°C
(a wok is the most suitable pan for
this recipe as you can easily slide the
tempura mixture into the pan).
(To check that the temperature of the oil
is hot enough, see method of Sea Bass
and Prawn Tempura with Ponzu Sauce
recipe on page 37.)

Take a small plate and grease it with a little
oil, then scoop out some of the seafood
mixture onto the small plate. Flatten the
mixture on the plate to make a small disc
(about 8cm in diameter). Gently slide the
disc of seafood mixture into the hot oil
by using chopsticks or a spoon.

Repeat this process until you have used
up all of the seafood mixture. Cook
each piece for about 2 minutes, turning
them over regularly. Be careful not to
overcrowd the pan when cooking the
tempura, as this will result in soggy
tempura. Each disc should have plenty
of room to move around in the pan.

Remove the cooked discs and drain on
kitchen paper. Serve immediately with
the dipping sauce.

JAPANESE POTATO SALAD

4 potatoes, each cut into 4
salt and white pepper, to taste
3 hard-boiled eggs, cooled and
  shelled
2 tablespoons soured cream
3–5 tablespoons Japanese
  mayonnaise (if not, use English
  mayonnaise whisked together
  with 1 egg yolk)
½ small onion, thinly sliced
½ cucumber, cut into thin
  matchsticks
1 carrot, cut into thin matchsticks
100g smoked ham, cooked cold
  unsmoked (streaky or back) bacon
  or cooked peeled prawns, diced
2 tablespoons teriyaki sauce (see
  recipe on page 37) (optional)

The Japanese are very good at importing dishes from elsewhere and improving them for their own palate. This dish is one of those. It is best served cold and is often served together with deep-fried crumbed dishes, such as Tonkatsu (Crumbed Pork), in Japan.

SERVES 4

Cook the potatoes in a pan of boiling water until they are just cooked. Drain well, then put the potatoes back into the pan and return to the heat for 1 minute to evaporate the excess water. Remove from the heat and mash or crush the potatoes and season with salt and white pepper (you can mash the potatoes until completely smooth or crush them leaving lumps, as you wish). Transfer the potatoes to a serving bowl.

Cut the eggs in half and separate the egg yolks and whites. Mash them into crumbles in two separate bowls.

Add the soured cream, mayonnaise and salt to taste to the potatoes and mix well. Add the onion, cucumber, carrot, ham (or bacon or prawns) and crumbled egg whites to the potato mixture and mix gently.

Drizzle the teriyaki sauce, if using, over the potato salad in crossing lines. Sprinkle the crumbled egg yolks over the salad and serve immediately or chill for about 1 hour before serving. Alternatively, store in an airtight container in the fridge and eat within 2 days.

GREEN BEANS AND FISHCAKES WITH SPICY MAYO

300g green beans or small asparagus
    spears, trimmed
a pinch of salt
3 sticks chikuwa fishcakes or
    Chinese fishcakes
2 tablespoons Japanese mayonnaise
    or salad cream
½–1 teaspoon grated garlic
1 teaspoon chilli paste
1 tablespoon sesame oil
1 tablespoon sesame seeds (optional)

This type of dish is eaten in Japan every day and everywhere. No specific Japanese name exists for these fishcakes but they are very tasty, easy and comforting. This recipe is pretty economical to make and is a great home cooking dish.

SERVES 4

Cook the green beans in a pan of boiling water with a pinch of salt added for about 5 minutes or until tender (2 minutes for the asparagus). Drain well. Cut the fishcakes on the diagonal into 1cm-wide pieces.

Mix the mayonnaise, grated garlic and chilli paste together in a small bowl. Set aside.

Heat the sesame oil in a frying pan and fry the green beans for 1 minute, then add the fishcake pieces and fry them together for a further 1 minute.

Turn the heat up to the highest setting and VERY quickly toss the mayonnaise mixture into the pan, then transfer the entire mixture to a serving plate. Sprinkle with the sesame seeds, if you wish, and serve immediately.

NANBAN MACKEREL

(MARINATED DEEP-FRIED MACKEREL)

440ml dashi stock (see recipe on
    page 32)
110ml soy sauce
110ml rice vinegar
4 tablespoons caster sugar
1–2 teaspoons dried chilli flakes or
    2 fresh red chillies, deseeded and
    finely chopped
1 onion, thinly sliced
1 carrot, thinly sliced
1 stick celery, thinly sliced
5cm piece fresh root ginger, peeled
    and thinly sliced, then cut into
    needle-thin sticks, or grated
4 large fresh mackerel fillets (about
    150g each), with skin on, washed
    and patted dry
120g plain flour
vegetable oil (at least 1 litre), for
    deep-frying

It is very important to make this dish at least half a day in advance and preferably leave it in the fridge overnight. By marinating this dish for a day or so, it makes sure that the mackerel fully absorbs the flavour from the sauce and the vegetables become properly pickled.

SERVES 4

Mix the dashi stock, soy sauce, rice vinegar, sugar and chilli together in a bowl. Add the prepared vegetables and ginger, stir to mix, then leave the mixture to infuse for about 30 minutes. Transfer the mixture to a flat or shallow container.

Cut the mackerel into large bite-size pieces. Dust the fish all over with the flour, shaking off the excess flour.

Heat the vegetable oil in a deep, heavy-based saucepan or a wok over a medium heat until it reaches 180°C. (To check that the temperature of the oil is hot enough, see method of Tonkatsu recipe on page 38.)

Deep-fry the fish in the hot oil for about 1–1½ minutes (depending on the thickness of the fillets) or until light golden in colour. As soon as the fish is cooked, remove it from the oil and drain on kitchen paper, then add the fish pieces to the marinade, turning them over and making sure every piece of fish is coated with the marinade.

Leave to cool, then cover tightly with cling film and chill in the fridge for at least 6 hours before serving. You can keep it up to 2 days in the fridge.

SALMON AND CHILLI MISO HOT POT

2 leeks, washed and cut into 2.5cm
  slices
1 large carrot
200g fresh shimeji mushrooms
2 litres dashi stock (see recipe on
  page 32)
8 small new potatoes
2 tablespoons normal miso paste
3 tablespoons white miso paste
1–2 teaspoons toh ban jan (Chinese
  chilli bean paste)
110ml sake
110ml mirin
1 tablespoon soy sauce
400g firm tofu, cut into 5cm cubes
25g butter
½ tablespoon vegetable oil
800g salmon fillet (with skin on), cut
  into 5cm cubes
salt and freshly ground black pepper,
  to taste
seven-spice chilli powder, to taste

This is a perfect winter home cooking dish. The mixture of white miso paste and chilli paste makes this dish unique and very warming. You can use white fish such as cod or haddock (with skin on), if you wish.

SERVES 4

Cut the leeks widthways into 2.5cm slices. Cut the carrot diagonally into 4 long sticks. Tear the shimeji mushrooms into chunks.

Put the dashi stock in a flameproof casserole dish or Japanese hot pot (nabe). Bring to the boil, then add the potatoes, leeks and carrot sticks and bring back to the boil. Reduce the heat and simmer for about 4–5 minutes or until the potatoes are only just tender.

Add both types of miso paste, the toh ban jan, sake, mirin, soy sauce, tofu and mushrooms, bring back to the boil and simmer for a further 4 minutes.

Meanwhile, heat a separate frying pan over a medium-high heat and add the butter and vegetable oil (the oil will stop the butter from burning). Once the butter is melted, add the salmon cubes and quickly sear the salmon with a pinch of salt and pepper for 2–3 minutes, turning the cubes around so that the salmon pieces are seared evenly all over.

Add the salmon cubes to the pan of stock and vegetables and cook for a further 2 minutes. Take the whole pot to the table to serve. Serve with seven-spice chilli powder on the side.

SEAFOOD CROQUETTES, JAPANESE-STYLE

30g butter
½ large onion, finely chopped
80g canned (drained) crabmeat or good-quality crabsticks, roughly chopped
80g cooked peeled prawns, roughly chopped
¼ teaspoon salt
¼ teaspoon white pepper
2 tablespoons dry or medium white wine
300g thick white sauce (made using 75g butter, 75g plain flour and 400ml milk) – see Cook's Tip
1–2 tablespoons extra-thick double cream
2 potatoes, boiled, drained, mashed and cooled
4 tablespoons plain flour
1 large egg, beaten
150g panko breadcrumbs
vegetable oil (at least 1 litre), for deep-frying
crispy salad leaves, lemon wedges and tonkatsu sauce, to serve

This is a great fusion dish that uses many Western ingredients. It is, however, still very important to use Japanese panko breadcrumbs and tonkatsu sauce for this recipe as these are the keys to success.

SERVES 4

Melt the butter in a frying pan, add the onion and fry until transparent. Add the seafood, salt, white pepper and white wine and cook until all the wine has evaporated. Transfer the seafood mixture to a large flat plate so that the mixture cools down quickly.

Make the white sauce (see Cook's Tip) – the texture of this thick white sauce should be more like soft dough rather than sauce. Once it's cooked, transfer it to a large flat plate to cool.

Mix the seafood, white sauce, cream and mashed potatoes together in a bowl. Cover and refrigerate for at least 1 hour, so that the mixture becomes firmer and easier to shape.

Take the mixture out of the fridge and divide it into 8–10 equal portions. Shape each portion into a cylinder/roll shape, about 5cm long. Dip each one first into the flour, then into the beaten egg and finally into the breadcrumbs, making sure each roll is coated all over with breadcrumbs.

Meanwhile, heat the vegetable oil in a deep, heavy-based saucepan or a wok over a medium heat until it reaches 180°C. (To check that the temperature of the oil is hot enough, see method of Tonkatsu recipe on page 38.)

Deep-fry the croquettes in the hot oil for about 1½–2 minutes or until golden brown and crisp. Remove and drain on kitchen paper. Serve the croquettes with the crispy salad leaves and lemon wedges and tonkatsu sauce on the side.

COOK'S TIP
To make the thick white sauce, melt the butter in a saucepan, then add the flour and cook gently, stirring, until well combined. Gradually add the milk, stirring constantly, then heat gently until the sauce comes to the boil and thickens, stirring. Simmer gently for 2 minutes, stirring until the sauce is silky smooth.

SESAME CRUMBED PRAWNS

FOR THE PRAWNS AND MARINADE

16 fresh tiger prawns in their shells
1 teaspoon grated (peeled) fresh
 root ginger
1 tablespoon finely chopped spring
 onions
1 tablespoon sake
1 teaspoon sesame oil
1 tablespoon cornflour
¼ teaspoon salt
¼ teaspoon white pepper

FOR THE BREADCRUMBS AND EGG COATING

100g panko breadcrumbs
1 tablespoon white sesame seeds
1 tablespoon black sesame seeds
1 large egg, beaten
vegetable oil (at least 1 litre),
 for deep-frying

FOR THE DIPPING SAUCE

2 tablespoons normal miso paste
4 tablespoons cold water
2 tablespoons mirin
1 tablespoon caster sugar
½ tablespoon grated (peeled)
 fresh root ginger

This is another very typical Japan-meets-West dish. Using large, juicy, plump fresh tiger prawns is the key to achieving the best results with this recipe. You can also try using vermicelli noodles or filo pastry instead of breadcrumbs for a unique version.

SERVES 4

For the prawns and marinade, shell, de-vein and wash the prawns, then pat them dry. Mix all the remaining ingredients together in a bowl to make the marinade, then, using your hands, rub the marinade mixture into the prawns, coating them completely to make sure all the flavours are absorbed into the prawns. Set aside.

For the breadcrumb mixture, mix the panko breadcrumbs and white and black sesame seeds together on a plate. Put the beaten egg into a shallow dish or bowl. Set aside.

Mix all the dipping sauce ingredients together, then heat them up in a saucepan and simmer for 3 minutes or heat in a microwave oven on high for 1 minute. Keep warm.

Meanwhile, heat the vegetable oil in a deep, heavy-based saucepan or a wok over a medium heat until it reaches 180°C. (To check that the temperature of the oil is hot enough, see method of Tonkatsu recipe on page 38.)

Dip the prawns into the beaten egg, then into the breadcrumb mixture, making sure each prawn is coated all over with the breadcrumbs.

Deep-fry the prawns in the hot oil for about 2–3 minutes or until golden and crispy (the cooking time will depend on the size of the prawns). Remove the prawns and drain on kitchen paper to remove excess oil. Serve the prawns with the miso and ginger dipping sauce on the side.

GINGER-FLAVOURED MEATBALLS

WITH SWEET AND SOUR SAUCE

FOR THE MEATBALLS

6 spring onions
200g minced beef
200g minced pork
1 tablespoon grated (peeled) fresh
    root ginger
1 egg
2 teaspoons sesame oil
1 tablespoon cornflour, plus extra for
    dusting
salt and white pepper, to taste
vegetable oil (at least 1 litre), for
    deep-frying
1 tablespoon sesame seeds, to
    garnish

FOR THE SWEET
AND SOUR SAUCE

110ml soy sauce
1 teaspoon instant dashi powder
3 tablespoons caster sugar
2 tablespoons sake
4 tablespoons rice vinegar
110ml cold water
1 tablespoon cornflour mixed with 3
    tablespoons cold water

Sweet and sour doesn't always mean a red-coloured sauce with pineapples! Japanese sweet and sour sauce can be your new discovery. Rice vinegar gives a kick of sourness to the sauce.

SERVES 4

Prepare the meatballs. Finely chop the white and green parts of the spring onions separately. Combine the minced beef and pork, the white part of the spring onions (reserve the green parts for the garnish), ginger, egg and sesame oil in a bowl. Add the 1 tablespoon cornflour, kneading it into the mixture until you feel the mixture is doughy and elastic. Season with salt and pepper.

Heat the vegetable oil in a wok or a deep, heavy-based saucepan over a medium heat until it reaches 180°C. (To check that the temperature of the oil is hot enough, see method of Tonkatsu recipe on page 38.)

Meanwhile, using a teaspoon, scoop the meat mixture into small portions and roll each portion into a small ball (about the size of a small ping-pong ball) using your hands. Dust each ball lightly with cornflour.

Carefully drop the meatballs into the hot oil and deep-fry for 2–3 minutes or until the surfaces becomes crispy. The cooking time will depend on the size of the meatballs. Remove the meatballs and drain on kitchen paper.

Put all the ingredients for the sauce, except the cornflour and water mixture, into a large frying pan. Turn the heat to medium. When the sauce starts to bubble, add the meatballs to the pan.

Cook the meatballs for 1 minute by shaking the pan. Pour the cornflour and water mixture into the pan and shake the pan over the heat (or stir) until the sauce becomes thick.

Transfer the meatballs and sauce to serving plates. Sprinkle the sesame seeds and reserved green parts of the spring onions over the top to garnish and serve.

NIKUJAGA

(BEEF AND POTATO STEW)

4 potatoes
600g rib-eye beef, thinly sliced
1 tablespoon vegetable oil
2 teaspoons sesame oil
1 large onion, thinly sliced
110ml soy sauce
4 tablespoons mirin
2–3 tablespoons caster sugar
2 carrots, cut into small, random-
    shaped bite-size pieces
1.5–2 litres hot water
1 teaspoon dashi powder
120g green beans, trimmed
a pinch of salt

This is one of the most commonly eaten dishes in Japan. You get the meat, potatoes and vegetables together in one pot and it is a truly comforting and nutritious dish.

SERVES 4

Peel and cut the potatoes into large bite-size pieces. Soak them in a bowl of cold water for 5 minutes, then drain well. Cut the beef slices into bite-size pieces (small enough to eat without further cutting).

Heat both the vegetable and sesame oils in a large saucepan over a medium heat. Add the onion and cook for 2 minutes, stirring constantly.

Push the onion to the edge of the pan, then add the beef pieces to the middle of the pan. Quickly mix the soy sauce, mirin and sugar together in a small bowl and pour over the beef in the pan. Cook as it is for 1 minute, then start mixing the onion and beef together.

Add the potatoes and carrots to the pan, then pour in 1.5 litres water and dashi powder. Turn the heat down to medium-low and simmer with a lid on for 15–20 minutes. Check and gently stir from time to time, making sure there is enough cooking liquid. If the mixture is becoming too dry, add some more hot water and mix.

Just before the beef mixture is ready, cook the green beans in a separate pan of boiling water with a pinch of salt added for about 3 minutes, then drain. Immediately transfer the green beans to the pan containing the beef mixture and cook for a further 1 minute, making sure the beans do not become overcooked. Spoon the beef mixture into serving bowls and serve.

CHICKEN 'TATSUTA AGE'-STYLE

3 tablespoons soy sauce
2 tablespoons sake
1 tablespoon mirin
1 tablespoon caster sugar
1 tablespoon grated (peeled) fresh
   root ginger
½ teaspoon grated garlic
500g skinless, boneless chicken thigh
   fillets, cut into large bite-size pieces
vegetable oil (at least 1 litre), for
   deep-frying
cornflour, for dusting
lemon or lime wedges, to serve

You may describe this as Japanese fried chicken. It's juicy, succulent and flavoursome. Simply serve with crispy iceberg lettuce for a tasty meal.

SERVES 4

Mix the soy sauce, sake, mirin, sugar and ginger together in a shallow dish, then add the chicken pieces, turning them over to make sure they are completely covered in the mixture. Cover and leave to marinate in the fridge for at least 2–3 hours or overnight. If you only have a couple of hours marinating time, rub the chicken well with the marinade so it absorbs the flavours more quickly.

Heat the vegetable oil in a deep, heavy-based saucepan or a wok over a medium heat until it reaches 170°C. (To check that the temperature of the oil is hot enough, see method of Tonkatsu recipe on page 38.)

Remove the chicken pieces from the marinade (discard the marinade) and dust them all over with cornflour, making sure each piece is well coated. Deep-fry the chicken pieces in the hot oil for about 2–3 minutes (depending on the size of the pieces) or until dark golden brown (but not burnt!) and crisp. Remove and drain on kitchen paper. Serve immediately with lemon or lime wedges.

STEAMED CHICKEN WITH SESAME SAUCE

FOR THE STEAMED CHICKEN

1 cucumber
salt and white pepper, to taste
4 spring onions, trimmed, roughly
    chopped
5cm piece fresh root ginger, peeled
    and thinly sliced
4 small dried shiitake mushrooms,
    soaked in sugared water (see
    Cook's Tip on page 91) and drained
300g boneless chicken fillets,
    preferably with skin on
1 teaspoon sesame oil
4 tablespoons sake
100ml vegetable oil, for shallow-
    frying

FOR THE SESAME SAUCE

4 tablespoons tahini paste
2 tablespoons soy sauce
2 tablespoons caster sugar
1 tablespoon rice vinegar
1–2 teaspoons chilli paste

COOK'S TIP
If you prefer, sprinkle the chicken with deep-fried shallots instead of the crispy fried chicken skin. In Japan, we do not regard the skin of chicken, fish, etc, as unhealthy (there is plenty of goodness in the skin, so we like to include it in many dishes).

I recommend this healthy dish to anyone who is on a diet and wants to lose weight by eating tasty and filling food. You will get extra benefit by using good-quality chicken for this dish.

SERVES 4

Preheat the oven to 240°C/fan 220°C/ Gas Mark 9. For the steamed chicken, slice the cucumber into thin sticks and place in a colander. Sprinkle some salt over the cucumber and leave for 5 minutes, then rinse off the salt. Drain the cucumber and pat dry with kitchen paper. Place on a serving plate or platter and set aside.

Place a large, double-layered piece of foil on the work surface. Place half of the spring onions, ginger and mushrooms on the foil and place the chicken on top. Place the remaining spring onions, ginger and mushrooms on top of the chicken. Season with the sesame oil and salt and white pepper.

Carefully wrap the chicken in the foil by folding nearly all around the edge of the foil to make a parcel. Make sure the sides are tightly closed but leave one side open and pour in the sake, then fold the opened side over to seal the ingredients completely inside the parcel. Place this on a baking tray and bake in the oven for about 15 minutes or until the chicken is just cooked.

Meanwhile, in a small bowl, mix together all the ingredients for the sesame sauce.

Remove the chicken from the oven and carefully open the foil. Pour 50ml of the cooking juices from the cooked chicken into the sauce mixture and mix well. The consistency of the sauce should be as thick as custard.

Discard the ginger and spring onions that were cooked with the chicken but keep the mushrooms and slice them very thinly. Remove and reserve the skin from the chicken. Leave the chicken to cool slightly, loosely covered with foil.

Finely chop the chicken skin. Heat the vegetable oil in a frying pan, add the chicken skin and fry until it becomes crispy all over.

Cut the chicken into 5mm-thick slices and lay the slices on top of the cucumber, together with the reserved sliced mushrooms. Pour the sesame sauce over the chicken and sprinkle the crispy chicken skin over the top. Serve. You may add ground black sesame seeds into the sauce for the colour and texture.

OYAKO-DONBURI

(CHICKEN AND EGG ON RICE)

220ml dashi stock (see recipe on
   page 32)
4 tablespoons soy sauce
2 tablespoons mirin
2 tablespoons caster sugar
1 tablespoon sake
1 onion, thinly sliced
200g skinless, boneless chicken thigh
   fillets, cut into 2cm cubes
6 eggs, lightly beaten
freshly cooked piping hot rice (a
   medium size bowlful of cooked
   rice per person), to serve
2 tablespoons finely chopped spring
   onions, to garnish
2–3 tablespoons red pickled ginder,
   drained
sansho pepper, to serve (optional)

'Oyako' – what a funny name! The word 'oya' means a parent and the word 'ko' means a child in Japanese. Indeed, the main ingredients for 'oyako' donburi are chicken and egg.

SERVES 4

Heat the dashi stock, soy sauce, mirin, sugar and sake together in a shallow, flat pan. Add the onion and chicken and simmer for 5–7 minutes or until the onion is thoroughly cooked.

Turn the heat up to medium-high, then gradually pour the beaten eggs into the pan, from the centre of the pan to the edges, using a swirling motion. When the eggs look half cooked, turn off the heat and leave the mixture for 1 minute. Do not mix.

Spoon the hot cooked rice into 4 individual bowls. Immediately scoop the egg and chicken mixture over the rice. Sprinkle the spring onions over the top and place a little red ginger in the middle to garnish. Serve with sansho pepper as a condiment, if you like.

KATSU-DONBURI

(CHICKEN KATSU AND EGG ON RICE)

330ml cold water
1 teaspoon instant dashi powder
1 onion, thinly sliced
4 tablespoons soy sauce
2 tablespoons mirin
2 tablespoons caster sugar
1 tablespoon sake
4 small portions chicken katsu (see recipe on page 118), sliced
4 eggs, lightly beaten
freshly cooked piping hot rice (a medium size bowlful of cooked rice per person), to serve
sansho pepper, to serve (optional)

Donburi is a very traditional and a much-loved dish enjoyed by many for lunch or dinner in Japan. Donburi is actually the name of the bowl used to serve the dish. It is larger than a rice bowl and slightly smaller than a noodle bowl. Anything is served on top of the rice served in the bowl and toppings vary to create a range of donburi dishes. Donburi is usually served with a simple miso soup and pickles, completing a very satisfying and filling meal. I will show you a selection of popular donburi dishes eaten in Japan in this section.

If you are on a diet, perhaps you must skip this recipe! But, if you want to give yourself a good burst of energy and enjoy a delicious and satisfying one-pot meal, nothing can beat Katsu-Donburi.

SERVES 4

Heat the water and instant dashi powder together in a large frying pan until simmering. Add the onion and simmer for 3 minutes or until the onion becomes soft.

Add the soy sauce, mirin, sugar and sake and simmer for a further 3 minutes over the lowest heat.

Turn the heat up to medium-high and add the sliced tonkatsu. Immediately after adding the pork, pour the beaten eggs evenly into the pan. Cook for a further 30 seconds or until the eggs are just beginning to set but are still runny. Be careful not to overcook the eggs, otherwise the tonkatsu pork will become dry.

Spoon the hot cooked rice into 4 individual bowls. Top with the tonkatsu and egg mixture. Serve immediately with sansho pepper on the side, if you like.

KAKIAGE-DONBURI

(KAKIAGE TEMPURA ON RICE)

330ml dashi stock (see recipe on
    page 32)
4 tablespoons mirin
4 tablespoons soy sauce
1/2 teaspoon caster sugar
1/2 teaspoon salt
freshly cooked piping hot rice
    (a medium size bowlful of cooked
    rice per person), to serve
4 discs of kakiage (see recipe on page
    98)
2 tablespoons grated (peeled) fresh
    root ginger
2 tablespoons grated daikon radish
    (optional)

This is a very casual way to eat tempura. Instead of cooking individual ingredients separately and serving the rice in a separate bowl, this is all made and served in one bowl. You may use leftover tempura from the night before. A microwave comes in very handy!

SERVES 4

Put the dashi stock, mirin, soy sauce, sugar and salt in a saucepan and stir to mix. Cook over a high heat until the mixture is boiling, then turn the heat down and simmer for about 10–15 minutes.

Spoon the hot cooked rice into 4 individual bowls. Place a whole disc of kakiage in each bowl. Pour the sauce into each bowl around the edge of the bowl, so that the kakiage stay dry and crispy.

Put a little pile of grated ginger in the middle of each disc of kakiage. If you wish to use the grated daikon radish, squeeze the water out as it is very watery and place the daikon next to the ginger. Serve.

CHICKEN KATSU CURRY

FOR THE CHICKEN KATSU

4 skinless, boneless chicken breast
fillets
60g plain flour
salt and white pepper, to taste
2 eggs
100–150g panko breadcrumbs
vegetable oil (at least 1 litre), for
  deep-frying
about 1.2kg freshly cooked piping
  hot rice (a medium size bowlful of
  cooked rice per person), to serve
4 tablespoons fukushin-zuke
  (Japanese red pickles always served
  with Japanese curry), drained, to
  serve

FOR THE CURRY SAUCE

2 tablespoons vegetable oil
1½ large onions, finely chopped
3 carrots, roughly chopped
2 garlic cloves, grated
2 chicken drumsticks, with skin on
220ml dry or medium white wine
2 litres boiling water
200g Japanese curry roux mix (see
  Cook's Tip)

About 1.2kg freshly cooked piping
  hot rice (a medium size bowlful of
  cooked rice per person to serve).
4 tablespoons Japanese fukushin-zuke
  red pickles
4 Japanese Jakkyo shallots, (always
  served with Japanese curry),
  drained, to serve.

**This is one of the most popular dishes amongst hungry and poor
students! It is delicious, filling and economical. There is something about
curry that always seems to whet your appetite.**

SERVES 4

First prepare the curry sauce. Heat the
vegetable oil in a large saucepan over a
medium-high heat. Add the onions,
carrots, garlic and chicken drumsticks
and cook for about 3 minutes, stirring
constantly and taking care not to let the
ingredients burn.

Add the white wine and cook for about
1 minute. Add the boiling water and
bring back to the boil, then turn the heat
down to medium-low and add the curry
roux mix, breaking it up as you go. Stir it
well until all the roux mix has dissolved.
Turn the heat down to low and simmer,
uncovered, for about 30 minutes, stirring
occasionally. Remove the chicken
drumsticks and set aside to cool for
another use (you may like to eat these
with salad or as a snack another time
– refrigerate once cold).

Meanwhile, as the curry sauce is
cooking, make the chicken katsu.
Butterfly the chicken breasts by scoring
each of them lengthways in the centre
about 5mm deep, so that the breasts can
be opened up wider and flatter. The aim
for this is to have an even thickness
throughout each breast.

Season the flour with a little salt and
pepper and put it on a plate. Put the eggs
into a shallow dish and beat them lightly.
Spread the breadcrumbs over a separate
plate or shallow dish.

Dip the butterflied chicken breasts first
in the flour, covering them all over, then
shake off any excess. Next, dip the
floured chicken into the beaten egg,
covering them completely, then finally
dip the chicken into the breadcrumbs,
ensuring each chicken breast is
completely covered with breadcrumbs.

Heat the vegetable oil in a deep, heavy-
based saucepan or a wok over a medium
heat until it reaches 170°C. (To check
that the temperature of the oil is hot
enough, see method of Tonkatsu recipe
on page 38.)

Slide the chicken portions into the hot oil.
Deep-fry the chicken for about 3–4 minutes
(depending on thickness), turning them
occasionally. Once the breadcrumb
coating becomes light golden brown in
colour, remove the chicken from the pan
and drain on kitchen paper. Leave it to
rest for 1 minute, then cut the chicken
into 1cm-thick slices.

Spoon the hot cooked rice into
4 individual flat bowls or plates. Place
the sliced chicken katsu on top. For each
portion, pour some curry sauce over
half of the chicken katsu, so that one
half of the chicken is covered with sauce
and the other half remains dry. Place
some fukushin-zuke pickles and lakkyo
pickles on the side of each portion and
serve immediately.

COOK'S TIPS

If you have any leftover curry sauce,
leave it to cool, then store in an airtight
container in the fridge for up to 5 days
or in the freezer for up to 3 months, and
use as required.

Japanese curry roux mix comes in solid
blocks like stock cubes. One box weighs
200g and contains what looks like giant
chocolate bars, each with 8 cubes of
roux mix connected. You can use as
many as you need and simply break
off each cube, then break up the cubes
before use.

GYU-DONBURI

(TERIYAKI-FLAVOURED BEEF ON RICE)

20g mangetout
a pinch of salt
330ml dashi stock (see recipe on
 page 32)
1 large onion, thinly sliced
3 tablespoons caster sugar
3 tablespoons soy sauce
2 tablespoons mirin
1 tablespoon sake
160g rib-eye beef (or fillet), thinly
 sliced
freshly cooked piping hot rice
 (a medium size bowlful of cooked
 rice per person), to serve
2–3 tablespoons red pickled ginger,
 drained, to serve

This is probably the cheapest way to eat beef in a dish in Japan. There are three major 'Gyu Don' chain restaurants and all of them are extremely popular. The price is very competitive and so is the taste. I have used mangetout to make it look pretty but the taste is still as fantastic without it.

SERVES 4

Blanch the mangetout in a small pan of boiling water with a pinch of salt added for 30 seconds, then rinse under cold water and drain. If you don't cool the mangetout straightaway, the colour will change to dark brownish green and it's important to retain the bright green colour. Thinly slice the mangetout diagonally and set them aside.

Heat the dashi stock in a large frying pan (a slightly deeper pan is ideal) over a medium heat. Add the onion and cook for 2 minutes.

Add the sugar, soy sauce, mirin and sake and stir to mix all the ingredients together, then cook for about 2–3 minutes. Add the beef slices and spread them out over the base of the pan. Do not mix them too much but let them cook as if you are poaching them. Cook for about 5 minutes or until the cooking liquid is reduced by about a quarter.

Spoon the hot cooked rice into 4 individual bowls. Pour the beef with the sauce over the rice. Sprinkle the sliced mangetout over the beef and place a little pickled ginger in the middle of each portion. Serve.

GYU-DONBURI:
A VERY SIMPLE BEEF DISH

1. Adding flavours of mirin, soy sauce and sugar to the base of stock, onion and beef.
2. Topping the dish with a garnish of mangetout and red pickled ginger.

1

MISO RAMEN

FOR THE NOODLES

2 tablespoons vegetable oil
120g pork belly or loin, thinly sliced
20g mangetout
80g canned sliced bamboo shoots
  (drained weight), drained or
  12 fresh (or canned, drained) baby
  corn, sliced diagonally
a pinch of salt
½ teaspoon white pepper
200g bean sprouts
500g fresh ramen noodle (if you
  can't get hold of fresh ones, use
  250g dried ones or about 600g
  pre-boiled ones instead)
2 teaspoons lah-yu or chilli-infused
  sesame oil (see Cook's Tip)
1–2 garlic cloves, grated
4 tablespoons finely chopped spring
  onions

FOR THE SOUP

1.2 litres ramen stock (see recipe on
  page 33)
2 tablespoons soy sauce
3–4 tablespoons normal miso paste
3 tablespoons white miso paste

Ramen noodle was originated in China. It has been brought into Japan and is re-pronounced in a Japanese way as 'rah-men'. The style and presentation of ramen noodle is very similar to Chinese noodles but it has been converted to the Japanese way and the flavour is distinctively different to the Chinese soup noodles. The most well-known and popular flavours of ramen noodle are the miso and sho-yu (soy sauce) ones in Japan.

Miso, raw garlic and chilli bring depth of flavour to the broth in this recipe and make it rich. Traditionally, miso ramen was most often eaten in the cooler northern parts of Japan because it is a warming dish. Pork is the perfect match for this soup but you may like to try chicken or prawns, if you wish.

SERVES 4

For the soup, heat the ramen stock in a large saucepan until it comes to the boil. Once the stock is boiling, add the soy sauce and both miso pastes and stir well until the miso paste melts completely. Turn the heat down to a simmer.

As the stock mixture is simmering, prepare the noodles. Heat the vegetable oil in a wok over a high heat, add the pork slices and stir-fry for 1 minute. Turn the heat down to medium, then add the mangetout and bamboo shoots (or baby corn) and season with a pinch of salt and the white pepper. Continue stir-frying by shaking the wok for another 2 minutes. Finally, turn the heat up to high again, add the bean sprouts and cook for 1 more minute. Remove from the heat.

Add the pork and vegetable mixture to the simmering stock mixture and cook for a further 2–3 minutes, then turn off the heat.

Meanwhile, bring a separate large pan of water to the boil. Add the fresh noodles and cook for about 2 minutes or according to the packet instructions. If you are using the dried noodles, they should take about 5–6 minutes to cook (or according to packet instructions). If you are using the pre-boiled noodles, just loosen them in some boiling water. Drain the noodles well.

Divide the hot noodles between 4 individual large noodle bowls. Pour the soup with all the meat and vegetables into each bowl, dividing the soup mixture evenly between the bowls. Drizzle a little lah-yu over each portion, then sprinkle the grated garlic and chopped spring onions over the top. Serve immediately.

COOK'S TIP
If you can't find lah-yu, you can instead use a mixture of sesame oil and chilli paste or dried chilli flakes – combine approximately 1 tablespoon sesame oil and $1/2$ teaspoon chilli paste (or add the chilli paste to suit your taste).

SHO-YU RAMEN

(SOY SAUCE FLAVOUR)

12 slices of cha-shu pork (see below on how to make it)

FOR THE CHA-SHU PORK

400g rolled pork shoulder joint
2 tablespoons vegetable oil
5cm piece fresh root ginger, peeled and thinly sliced
3–4 spring onions, cut into 5cm long pieces
2 tablespoons sake
440ml boiling water
4 tablespoons soy sauce
2 tablespoons caster sugar

FOR THE NOODLES AND SOUP

500g fresh ramen noodles (if you can't get hold of fresh ones, use 250g dried ones or about 600g pre-boiled ones instead)
1.2 litres ramen stock (see recipe on page 33)
4–5 tablespoons soy sauce
120g menma (pickled bamboo shoots, sold in bottles), drained
2 hard-boiled eggs, cooled, shelled and cut in half lengthways
8 slices (about 100g) kamaboko (ready-cooked Japanese fishcakes)
1 nori sheet (about 19cm square), cut into 8 even pieces
2 tablespoons finely chopped spring onions
½ teaspoon white pepper
2 teaspoons sesame oil

As sho-yu (soy sauce) is used in most Japanese dishes, this popular noodle dish is the most familiar one to all Japanese people. You can add your own toppings or seasonings to vary the flavour, if you like.

SERVES 4

First prepare and cook the cha-shu pork. Make sure the rolled pork joint is tied up securely. Heat the vegetable oil in a wok until it is very hot and just smoking, then add the ginger, spring onions and pork and sear the surface of the pork all over by turning it frequently until the meat becomes brown.

Pour the sake over the pork, then add the boiling water, soy sauce and sugar. Turn the heat down to the lowest setting, then cover and simmer for about 30 minutes. Turn the pork over from time to time to make sure the flavours are absorbed evenly into the pork.

Transfer the pork to a heatproof container and half-cover with the lid, then leave the pork to cool a little. While the pork is still warm (but not hot), cut the pork joint into even slices just before serving. You will need 12 slices of the pork for this recipe, so any leftover pork can be cooled completely and stored in an airtight container in the fridge for up to 5 days (see also Cook's Tips).

Meanwhile, prepare the noodles and soup. Bring a large pan of water to the boil. Add the fresh noodles and cook for about 2 minutes or according to the packet instructions. If you are using the dried noodles, they should take about 5–6 minutes to cook (or according to packet instructions). If you are using the pre-boiled noodles, just loosen them in some boiling water. Drain the noodles well.

As the noodles are cooking, heat the stock in a separate saucepan until it is boiling. Add the soy sauce and bring the soup back to the boil.

Divide the hot noodles between 4 individual noodle bowls. Pour some soup into each bowl, dividing it evenly between the bowls. Lay the slices of cha-shu pork, menma, boiled egg halves, kamaboko slices and nori pieces on top of the noodles, dividing evenly. Finally, sprinkle each portion with spring onions and a little white pepper and drizzle with the sesame oil. Serve immediately.

COOK'S TIPS
Menma and kamaboko can both be purchased from Japanese shops.

LEI-MEN

(CHILLED RAMEN NOODLE)

FOR THE NOODLES

1 tablespoon vegetable oil
2 eggs, beaten with a little salt
4 iceberg lettuce leaves
160g fresh egg noodles
1 cucumber, cut into matchsticks
200g smoked ham, cut into thin
   strips
2 tablespoons red pickled ginger,
   drained
2 teaspoons Japanese mustard

FOR THE SAUCE

110ml rice vinegar
110ml soy sauce
1 tablespoon mirin
2 tablespoons caster sugar
1 tablespoon lemon juice
1 teaspoon instant dashi powder
   dissolved in 1 tablespoon hot
   water
1 teaspoon sesame oil

During the hot summer season, Japanese people love eating this dish. Other variations in the toppings can be used for this dish, such as fishcakes, cha-shu pork, blanched mangetout or any crunchy lettuce leaves.

SERVES 4

For the noodles, heat the vegetable oil in a frying pan until hot. Pour half of the lightly salted beaten eggs into the pan, spread the egg mixture over the base of the pan and cook for 10 seconds, then flip over and cook the other side for another 10 seconds. Remove from the pan to a plate. Cook the remaining egg mixture in the same way. Leave it to cool, then slice thinly.

Soak the lettuce leaves in a bowl of ice-cold water for 5 minutes, then drain thoroughly, pat dry and slice the leaves thinly. This way the lettuce remains very crispy.

Bring a large pan of water to the boil. Add the noodles and cook for about 2–3 minutes or according to the packet instructions. Drain the noodles, then rinse under cold running water until the noodles are completely cold. Drain them thoroughly.

Mix all the sauce ingredients together in a small bowl.

Divide the cold noodles between 4 individual plates or bowls and top each portion with the slices of cooked egg mixture, the cucumber, ham and lettuce (keeping each topping separate), dividing them evenly between each portion. Pour the sauce over the whole dish, dividing it evenly, then put the red pickled ginger in the centre. Top each serving with 1/2 teaspoon mustard and serve immediately.

COOK'S TIPS

Any leftover cha-shu pork can be stored as indicated and served cold with some mustard, chilli paste or soy sauce, or it can be added to other dishes such as fried rice or noodles or used for sandwiches.

YAKI-UDON

(STIR-FRIED UDON NOODLE)

1 tablespoon vegetable oil

300g pork belly or loin, thinly sliced, then cut into 3-cm wide pieces

½ large onion, sliced

8 large cabbage leaves, cut into 3-cm wide pieces

1 carrot, cut into thick matchsticks

1 green pepper, deseeded and cut into thick matchsticks

600g steamed udon noodles

110ml ready-made or homemade tonkatsu sauce (see recipe on page 38)

2 teaspoons soy sauce

1 teaspoon tomato purée

2 tablespoons ao-nori (dried green seaweed sprinkles)

4 tablespoons bonito flakes

The yellow egg noodles traditionally used for this dish are often seen in street fairs in Japan. Udon noodles are a suitable alternative and are equally tasty, as this recipe demonstrates well.

SERVES 4

Please note, with this recipe, it is easier to cook two portions first and then repeat again for the remaining two portions. Otherwise, the pan will be too crowded and it will be hard to fry the noodles properly.

Heat the vegetable oil in a large frying pan or a wok over a medium heat. Add the pork and onion and stir-fry for 2 minutes. Add the cabbage, carrot and green pepper and stir-fry for a further 2 minutes.

Add the noodles and toss to mix well with the other ingredients. Continue stir-frying, then pour in the tonkatsu sauce, soy sauce and tomato purée and stir-fry for a further 1 minute or until the mixture is hot and the noodles are coated all over with the sauce.

Transfer the noodle mixture to individual plates, dividing it evenly. Sprinkle some ao-nori and bonito flakes over each portion and serve.

DEEP-FRIED TOFU WITH BLACK SESAME PASTE

100g green beans, trimmed
a pinch of salt
3 tablespoons black sesame seeds
1 tablespoon caster sugar
3 tablespoons soy sauce
3 tablespoons mirin
400g Chinese deep-fried tofu
  (Chinese tofu is different to
  Japanese tofu)
1 tablespoon sesame oil
1 tablespoon vegetable, corn or
  sunflower oil

Slightly sweet black sesame paste is a perfect match for golden deep-fried tofu, and bright green beans add extra colour and texture. Deep-fried tofu is crispy on the outside and juicy on the inside and you will enjoy the real tofu flavour in every bite of this dish.

SERVES 4

Cook the green beans in a pan of boiling water with a pinch of salt added for 3 minutes, then drain well. Leave to cool, then cut into 2.5cm lengths. Set aside.

Lightly toast the black sesame seeds in a dry frying pan over a low heat to release the flavour (this will only take a few minutes), then remove from the heat and grind the seeds to a rough powder using a pestle and mortar. Add the sugar, soy sauce and mirin and mix well. Set aside.

Bring a large pan of water to the boil. Add the deep-fried tofu and blanch for 2–3 minutes, pressing the tofu occasionally to squeeze the oil out, especially as Chinese deep-fried tofu can be very oily. Drain the deep-fried tofu in a colander, then squeeze the water out from the tofu. Cut the tofu into large bite-size pieces.

Heat the sesame and vegetable oils in the saucepan you used for blanching the deep-fried tofu over a medium heat. Add the tofu pieces and quickly toss them in the oil for 2 minutes, turning the tofu pieces constantly. Turn off the heat, then add the green beans and black sesame paste and toss together to mix well. Serve.

MABO TOFU

(TOFU WITH SPICY RED MISO PORK)

FOR THE TOFU

400g silken tofu
a pinch of salt
2 tablespoons vegetable oil
½ leek, washed and finely chopped
1 garlic clove, finely chopped
200g minced pork
½ teaspoon white pepper
2–3 teaspoons toh ban jan (Chinese chilli bean paste)
a small handful of fresh coriander leaves

FOR THE RED MISO SAUCE

2 tablespoons miso paste (preferably 1 tablespoon normal miso paste and 1 tablespoon red miso paste combined – this mixture will give a better flavour)
2 tablespoons sake
2 tablespoons mirin
1½ tablespoons soy sauce
1½ tablespoons caster sugar
165ml cold water
1 teaspoon cornflour
1 tablespoon sesame oil

This is one of the most well-known and popular dishes that has originated in China and is now very popular in Japan. The original Chinese recipe has been altered to better suit the Japanese palate by using Japanese miso paste.

SERVES 4

Put all the ingredients for the red miso sauce in a small bowl and mix them together well. Set aside.

Prepare the tofu. Cut the tofu into 2cm cubes. Bring a medium pan of water to the boil and add a pinch of salt. Slowly slide the tofu into the pan and boil gently until all the pieces of tofu start floating. This way the excess water will be removed and the tofu pieces will become firmer, ensuring that they keep their shape more easily when you stir-fry them later. Drain the tofu in a colander and set aside, leaving the water to drip away.

Heat the vegetable oil in a wok over a medium-high heat. When the oil is hot, add the leek and garlic and quickly stir-fry them for 1 minute. Add the minced pork and white pepper and mix well, then flatten the meat mixture over the base of the wok. Stir-fry the mixture, constantly breaking up the minced meat up as you go. Add the toh ban jan and stir-fry for about 1 minute.

Stir the red miso sauce mixture well, then add to the wok. Mix the sauce and pork together well, then add the tofu. Carefully and gently mix the tofu with the pork mixture, taking care not to break the tofu. Cook for about 2 minutes, mixing gently by scooping from the bottom of the pan then folding over.

Transfer the mixture to a large serving bowl or plate. Sprinkle with coriander leaves and serve with steamed rice.

TOFU BAG FILLED WITH PORK AND EGG

FOR THE TOFU BAGS AND FILLING

4 sheets of deep-fried tofu, about
   20g each
100g minced pork
a pinch of salt
¼ carrot, finely chopped
2 spring onions, finely chopped
1 teaspoon grated (peeled) fresh root
   ginger
½ tablespoon cornflour
4 eggs
100g green beans, trimmed

FOR THE STOCK

330ml dashi stock (see recipe on
   page 32)
2 tablespoons sake
2 tablespoons caster sugar
2 tablespoons soy sauce

This dish is a typical example of the home cooking dishes. It's juicy and has different textures from each ingredient that go very well with plain rice.

SERVES 4

For the tofu bags and filling, cook the tofu sheets in a pan of boiling water for 1 minute to remove the oil, then drain. Gently squeeze the water out, taking care not to tear the sheets. Cut the tofu sheets in half and open them up. You now have 8 tofu bags. Set aside.

Mix the minced pork, salt, carrot, spring onions, ginger and cornflour together in a bowl using your hands. Divide the mixture into 4 equal portions.

Mix all the ingredients for the stock together in a large pan and bring it to the boil, then reduce the heat to a simmer.

Fill 4 of the tofu bags with the pork mixture, dividing it evenly. Secure the openings with cocktail sticks. Crack an egg into each of the 4 remaining tofu bags and secure the openings with cocktail sticks, taking care not to let the eggs spill from the bags. Now you have eight little tofu parcels.

Add all the parcels to the simmering stock in the pan and cook over a low heat, partially covered, for 20–25 minutes or until the tofu bags have soaked up most of the cooking liquid but some cooking liquid is left so that the tofu bags remain juicy.

Meanwhile, cook the green beans in a separate pan of boiling water for about 5 minutes. Drain and keep warm.

When the tofu bags are cooked, remove and discard the cocktail sticks and cut each one in half. Place one pork tofu bag (in two halves) and one egg tofu bag (in two halves) in each of 4 individual serving bowls.

Add the cooked green beans to the remaining cooking liquid in the pan and cook for about 1 minute. Spoon the beans on top of the tofu bags and pour the cooking liquid over the top. Serve immediately.

SILKEN TOFU WITH SESAME SALMON TOPPING

400g silken tofu
a little salt, for sprinkling
2 salmon fillets (about 150g each),
  with skin on
4 tablespoons vegetable oil
2 tablespoons toasted sesame oil
1 bunch spring onions, finely
  chopped
½ teaspoon toh ban jan (Chinese
  chilli bean paste)
4 tablespoons soy sauce
2 tablespoons mirin

For this recipe, I'm using freshly cooked salmon fillet, but if you are in a hurry or don't have fresh salmon, you can substitute with canned red salmon. It will still be surprisingly good.

SERVES 4

Cut the tofu into large cubes and cook the tofu cubes in a pan of boiling water for about 4–5 minutes. Drain the tofu in a colander and set aside, leaving the water to drip away as the tofu cools down.

Preheat the grill to medium. Sprinkle a little salt over the salmon fillets, place them, skin-side up, on the rack in a grill pan and grill for about 3 minutes. Turn over and grill for a further 4–5 minutes or until the salmon is just cooked and the skin is crispy. Remove from the grill and leave the salmon until it is cool enough to flake using your hands. Once cool enough, peel off and reserve the skin before flaking the fish. Set the flaked fish aside.

Place the two pieces of salmon skin (crispy-side down so the inside of the skin is on top) on the rack in the grill pan and grill for a minute or so until crispy. Remove and cool slightly, then break the crispy skin into small pieces and set aside to use as the garnish.

Reheat the tofu either in a microwave on HIGH for 2 minutes or steam it over a pan of simmering water for 10 minutes, until it is hot. If more water still comes out, carefully drain it away.

Meanwhile, heat the vegetable and sesame oils in a small saucepan over a medium-low heat. Reserve 1 tablespoon of the green part of the chopped spring onions, then add the remaining spring onions to the pan. Cook for 1 minute, then add the toh ban jan, soy sauce and mirin and cook for a further 1 minute.

Divide the hot tofu between 4 serving plates. Place the flaked salmon on top of the tofu, then pour the oil and spring onion mixture over the salmon. Sprinkle the reserved green spring onion and pieces of crispy salmon skin over the top and serve.

GOURMET DISHES

SCALLOPS WITH CREAMY SPICY SAUCE ON SUSHI RICE

FOR THE SCALLOPS AND RICE

4 large or 8 small fresh scallops in
    their shells (sashimi-quality)
vegetable oil, for greasing
360g prepared sushi rice (see recipe
    on page 35)
2 teaspoons shredded nori
4 teaspoons flying fish roe
1 lemon or lime, cut into wedges

FOR THE CREAMY SPICY SAUCE

2 large egg yolks
½ teaspoon salt
a little white pepper
1 tablespoon rice vinegar
150ml vegetable oil
1 tablespoon chilli paste or toh ban
    jan (Chinese chilli bean paste)

This is my signature dish. I teach this dish in my gourmet course.
Every time people taste this dish, everyone goes quiet as they are
thoroughly enjoying the whole experience of the flavour, texture and
appearance. Just follow the recipe and you will find it very easy to
prepare this sophisticated dish at home.

SERVES 4

First make the creamy spicy sauce.
Beat the egg yolks in a bowl, then add
the salt, a little white pepper and the
rice vinegar. Gradually whisk in the
vegetable oil, a little at a time, making
sure the sauce doesn't separate. Whisk
in the chilli paste. The consistency of
the sauce should be like slightly runny
mayonnaise. Set aside.

For the scallops and rice, remove
(shuck) the scallops from their shells,
then cut away and discard the soft, grey,
beard-like fringe and black intestinal
bag from each one. Rinse the scallops
in cold water and drain well. Cut the
scallop meat into 1cm chunks. Scrub
the lower shells (with rounded sides)
thoroughly in cold water and reserve.
(Discard the flat top shells.)

Preheat the grill to medium. Brush
the inside of each scallop shell with
vegetable oil to prevent the rice from
sticking. Place a quarter of the prepared
sushi rice into each shell (or an eighth,
if using 8 smaller scallops).

Cover the rice with the shredded nori,
lay the flying fish roe on top, followed
by the chunks of scallop meat. Place the
assembled scallop shells on the rack in a
grill pan.

Spoon the creamy spicy sauce over the
top of the scallops, making sure the
sauce is covering the filling completely.
Grill the assembled scallops until the
tops turn slightly golden brown (it is
important not to overcook the scallops).

Place the grilled scallops on serving
plates and serve them with lemon or
lime wedges on the side. If the shells
are unstable, place a small lump of salt
under each one to keep them in place.

COOK'S TIP
Flying fish roe is available from
Japanese fishmongers.

PRAWN CAKES IN CLEAR BROTH

FOR THE PRAWN CAKES

200g fresh peeled prawns
100g skinless white fish fillets, such as sea bass, sea bream or cod
1 whole egg
½ teaspoon salt
2 tablespoons cornflour
½ teaspoon baking powder
4 large fresh shiitake mushrooms, thinly sliced
4 spring onions, thinly sliced diagonally
a handful of watercress, roughly chopped
1–2 teaspoons wasabi paste

FOR THE BROTH

1 litre dashi stock (see recipe on page 32)
110ml sake
2 tablespoons soy sauce
1 tablespoon mirin
a pinch of salt

The key to success with this dish is to get the right smooth and elastic texture with the prawn and fish mixture, then all you do is to poach the prawn cakes in the broth. This is such a simple recipe but it is slightly more sophisticated than an ordinary soup.

SERVES 4

Prepare the prawn cakes. Chop the prawns and white fish as finely as possible, then press them through a sieve or a fine mesh colander. If you like to have a bit of texture in your fishcakes, just press the white fish through the sieve, not the prawns. Put the prawns and fish in a bowl. Add the egg yolk, salt, cornflour and baking powder and mix together well using your hands until the texture becomes smooth and elastic. If you have a food processor, you can do all of the above in the food processor. Set aside.

Heat all the broth ingredients together in a large pan. Once it reaches the boil, add the shiitake mushrooms and spring onions.

Next you need to poach the prawn and fish mixture in the broth mixture. Dividing the mixture into 4 equal portions and using two tablespoons, scoop out the prawn/fish mixture, shaping the scoops into round balls – you should have 4 round balls in total.

Gently slide each fishcake into the simmering broth. Repeat this until you have used up all the prawn/fish mixture.

Reduce the heat to a simmer and cook the fishcakes for 5–6 minutes or until they all rise up and float around in the broth. Add the watercress and turn up the heat to high for 30 seconds, then turn off the heat.

Place one fishcake in the centre of 4 individual bowls and pour the broth mixture over the top, dividing it evenly. The tops of the fishcakes should not be covered with the broth. Place a little wasabi paste on top of each fishcake. Serve immediately.

COOK'S TIP
This dish looks even more special if you serve it in dark soup bowls.

SEARED TUNA WITH PONZU-ONION DRESSING

220ml ponzu sauce (see recipe on
   page 37)
2 teaspoons caster sugar
2 tablespoons sesame oil
½ onion, very finely chopped or
   grated
600g fresh sashimi-quality tuna
1 tablespoon vegetable oil
1 tablespoon toasted sesame seeds,
   for sprinkling

This is the perfect starter for a smart dinner party – if you have a large budget! You can prepare everything in advance and then all you have to do is to slice the tuna and dish up just before serving. For vegetarians, why not serve sliced silken tofu with the same dressing and garnish with deep-fried shallots?

SERVES 4

Put the ponzu sauce, sugar, sesame oil and onion in a bowl and mix together. Cover and refrigerate for at least 1 hour before serving to allow the flavours to blend and infuse together.

Cut the tuna into 4 even slices or pieces – each slice or piece should be about 2.5cm thick. (If you can only buy the tuna steak part of the fish, try to choose the thick piece.)

Heat a frying pan until very hot. Brush the vegetable oil over the pieces of tuna, making sure all the surfaces are covered. Quickly sear the tuna pieces in the hot pan, turning them over and making sure all sides are seared – sear each side for about 20 seconds and be careful not to overcook the fish. (If you like very rare, just 10 seconds for each side)

Remove the dressing mixture from the fridge. Dip each piece of freshly cooked tuna into the cold dressing mixture so that the tuna stops cooking immediately and absorbs the flavour well. Leave the tuna pieces to marinate in the dressing for up to 1 hour in the fridge. The ideal marinating time is 15–30 minutes. If you leave the tuna to marinate in the dressing for too long, it will become cured or cooked.

Slice the tuna into 1cm-thick slices and arrange the slices on individual serving plates. Pour the dressing over the tuna, sprinkle with the sesame seeds and serve with some crunchy salad leaves. It is best to serve this dish at a cool room temperature, not ice-cold straight out of the fridge.

KAKIFULAI

(DEEP-FRIED OYSTERS) WITH JAPANESE SALSA

FOR THE OYSTERS

20 large fresh oysters in their shells
2 tablespoons sake
15g dried wakame seaweeds
20 endive leaves
120g plain flour
2 eggs, beaten
150g panko breadcrumbs
vegetable oil (at least 1 litre), for
    deep-frying

FOR THE SPICY PONZU SAUCE

4 tablespoons soy sauce
1 tablespoon rice vinegar
2 tablespoons lemon juice
½ large onion, finely chopped
2 fresh red chillies, deseeded and
    finely chopped
a pinch of salt
a pinch of white pepper
1 large tomato, finely chopped
a handful of fresh flat-leaf parsley,
    finely chopped

Put all the sauce ingredients, except the chopped tomato and parsley, in a small bowl and mix well. Cover and refrigerate for 30 minutes. Set the tomato and parsley aside.

For the oysters, remove (shuck) the oysters from their shells (taking care not to spill any of the juice from inside the shells). Drain the oyster juice into a bowl, add the sake and stir to mix. Add the oysters to this mixture, stir to mix,

As oysters are not considered a luxury ingredient in Japan, people often eat them at home. These deep-fried oysters served with a tasty sauce create a presentable and appealing dish.

SERVES 4

then leave to marinate for 5 minutes.

Grind the wakame seaweeds using a pestle and mortar to form fine crumbs. Wash and dry the endive leaves and keep them in the fridge covered with slightly damp kitchen paper in the fridge (the leaves become extra crispy if stored this way).

Put the flour into one shallow dish. Put the beaten eggs into another shallow dish and put the breadcrumbs into a third one. Add the wakame seaweed crumbs to the breadcrumbs and mix well.

First, toss the oysters in the flour, shaking off the excess, then dip the oysters in the beaten egg, then in the breadcrumb mixture, making sure each oyster is completely coated with breadcrumbs. If you are not cooking the oysters straightaway, place them on a plate and keep in the fridge until you are ready to deep-fry them (they will keep for a few hours).

Heat the vegetable oil in a deep, heavy-based saucepan or a wok over a medium heat until it reaches 180°C. (To check

that the temperature of the oil is hot enough, see method of Tonkatsu recipe on page 38.)

Deep-fry the oysters (straight from the fridge) in the hot oil in batches (making sure the pan doesn't get too crowded) for about 2 minutes at the most, depending on the size of the oysters. Do not leave the oysters in the oil until dark brown or they will be overcooked. The colour of the oysters should be light golden when you take them out – they will still continue to cook slightly and go slightly darker in colour as they sit draining on kitchen paper.

Add the chopped tomato and parsley to the chilled sauce mixture. Spoon the sauce into 4 small serving bowls (which will be placed in the centre of the plates), dividing evenly.

Lay 5 endive leaves on each serving plate, arranged like flower petals, and place 1 deep-fried oyster onto each leaf. Place the small bowls of dipping sauce in the centre of the plates and serve immediately.

TRIPLE JAPANESE MUSHROOM SALAD WITH YUZU DRESSING

FOR THE SALAD

200g assorted fresh Japanese
  mushrooms such as shiitake, enoki
  and shimeji
20g butter
1 garlic clove, grated
200g assorted crunchy salad leaves
40g toasted walnuts, roughly
  crushed or chopped
60g cottage cheese, goat cheese or
  feta cheese (roughly crumbled)
2 tablespoons snipped fresh chives

FOR THE YUZU (JAPANESE LIME) DRESSING

4 tablespoons yuzu (Japanese lime)
  juice
3 tablespoons soy sauce
1 teaspoon soft brown sugar
½ teaspoon finely ground black
  pepper
4 tablespoons grape seed oil

Three different types of mushrooms give you a variety of textures and flavours in this dish and they all combine perfectly with the distinctive flavour of yuzu (Japanese lime). Yuzu can be used as a garnish, for sauces or as a subtle flavouring, in the same way that you might use a lemon or lime. It's not easy to obtain the fresh fruits but most Japanese shops stock bottles of yuzu concentrate.

SERVES 4

Put all the ingredients for the yuzu dressing in a large bowl and whisk together until thoroughly mixed. Set aside.

Prepare the mushrooms for the salad – dust them with a damp cloth and cut or tear them into large bite-size pieces. Blanch the mushrooms in a pan of boiling water for 15 seconds, then drain well.

Quickly heat a large frying pan and add the butter. Once the butter is melted, add the garlic and all the mushrooms and sauté them over a high heat for about 2–3 minutes, shaking the pan from time to time.

As soon as the mushrooms are cooked, transfer them to the bowl of dressing. Toss to mix well.

Line a serving dish with the crunchy salad leaves. Spoon the mushroom mixture on top of the lettuce. Sprinkle the walnuts, cottage cheese and chives over the mushrooms and serve.

TOFU SHIRAAE SALAD

FOR THE SALAD

10g dried shiitake mushrooms
220ml warm water
½ teaspoon caster sugar
1 tablespoon soy sauce
1 tablespoon mirin
¼ teaspoon salt, plus 2 pinches of
  salt
1 carrot
150g fresh spinach leaves, rinsed
150g frozen edamame beans
  (young soya beans)
1 sheet of deep-fried tofu (about 20g)
20g dried apricots

FOR THE SHIRAAE DRESSING

200g silken tofu
1 tablespoon normal miso paste
1 teaspoon tahini paste
1 tablespoon caster sugar
1 tablespoon mirin
2 teaspoons soy sauce
a pinch of salt
1 tablespoon rice vinegar (optional)

Tofu is used for many dishes in Japan. One of its popular uses is to make sauces. The creaminess and richness of tofu makes a perfect sauce for vegetables, as I demonstrate in this delicious recipe. Try using different vegetables, depending on what is in season.

SERVES 4

For the salad, first soak the mushrooms in the warm water with the sugar added. Leave to soak for 2 hours, then drain, reserving 50ml of the soaking liquid and the mushrooms separately. Remove and discard the mushroom stalks. Put the mushroom caps, reserved soaking liquid, soy sauce, mirin and ¼ teaspoon salt in a pan and cook for about 5–6 minutes or until most of the liquid has evaporated. Remove from the heat and leave the mushrooms to cool, then slice them thinly.

Meanwhile, for the shiraae dressing, wrap the silken tofu in a muslin cloth or kitchen paper and squeeze out as much water as possible. Break up the tofu in a bowl. Add all the remaining ingredients for the dressing and mix together well. Set aside.

Cut the carrot into 4cm-long thin sticks. Bring a pan of water to the boil, add a pinch of salt, then add the carrots and boil for 2 minutes. Using a slotted spoon, remove the carrots to a plate and set aside. Add the spinach and cook for 20 seconds, then drain and rinse under cold running water until the spinach

becomes cold. Drain well, squeezing the water out completely. Set aside.

Fill the same pan with water, add a pinch of salt and bring to the boil. Add the edamame beans, bring back to the boil and cook for 3 minutes. Drain and rinse under cold running water, then drain again. Take the beans out of their pods; discard the pods.

Pour some boiling water over the deep-fried tofu in a dish, drain, then pour over cold water to cool the tofu, then drain again. Squeeze the water out, then thinly slice the tofu. Slice the dried apricots very thinly.

Pat all the cooked vegetables dry with kitchen paper and place them in a serving dish with the deep-fried tofu and apricot slices. Pour over the shiraae dressing and gently toss everything together to mix. Serve.

COOK'S TIP
If you cannot find edamame beans, you can use about 115g frozen podded broad beans or green peas (podded weight) instead. Cook as directed.

BEETROOT, ASPARAGUS AND MOZZARELLA WITH TAMA-MISO

(EGG-MISO)

FOR THE SALAD

4 fresh medium beetroots
8 large asparagus spears
a pinch of salt
200g mozzarella cheese
a handful of small watercress sprigs

FOR THE TAMA-MISO

100g white miso paste
2 egg yolks
1 tablespoon sake
1 tablespoon mirin
1 teaspoon soy sauce
1½ tablespoons caster sugar
2 tablespoons warm dashi stock
   (see recipe on page 32)
2 tablespoons double cream

This is a substantial salad that can either be served as a side dish or as a starter. Just remember to make sure the tama-miso sauce is a smooth and velvety texture.

SERVES 4

To make the tama-miso, put all the ingredients, except the dashi stock and cream, in a small saucepan and simmer, stirring constantly, over a low heat for 3 minutes or until the egg yolk is just cooked. Turn the heat off, then press the mixture through a fine sieve. Cool, then refrigerate. This mixture can be kept in the fridge in an airtight container for up to 5 days.

Make the salad. Cook the beetroots in a pan of boiling water for about 1 hour or until they become soft enough to easily put a cocktail stick through. Drain well and leave to cool. (Beetroot takes a long time to cook in a normal pan by this method, so the process will be quicker if you use a pressure cooker. Alternatively, you can use ready-cooked beetroots, but not the pickled ones.)

Trim the asparagus spears and peel the bottom ends. Cook the asparagus in a pan of boiling water with a pinch of salt added for 3 minutes or until just cooked (the asparagus should retain some crunchiness). Rinse under cold running water, drain, then pat dry. Cut the asparagus spears into 3cm lengths. Slice the mozzarella cheese into chunks

2 x 3cm in size. Peel the beetroots, then cut each one into 8 segments.

Put the tama-miso in a small bowl, then pour in 1 tablespoon of the warm dashi stock, stirring constantly. Pour in 1 tablespoon of the cream, stirring constantly. Check the consistency of the sauce – if it is the consistency of condensed milk there is no need to add any more dashi stock and cream, but if it is still too thick, add more of the remaining dashi stock and cream, little by little, until you have the correct consistency.

Arrange the asparagus, beetroot and mozzarella in 4 individual wide, flat bowls (soup or dessert bowls are ideal) and pour the tama-miso sauce over the vegetables. Garnish with the watercress sprigs.

CALAMARI AND BAMBOO SHOOT SALAD

WITH SPICY MISO DRESSING

FOR THE SALAD

200g fresh squid (calamari) –
   preferably large, thick ones
4 tablespoons cornflour
½ teaspoon salt, plus a pinch
½ teaspoon white pepper, plus a
   pinch
1 tablespoon vegetable oil
1 teaspoon sesame oil
140g canned bamboo shoots
   (drained weight), rinsed, drained
   and sliced
2 garlic cloves, grated
2 spring onions, trimmed
100g mixed salad leaves
4 teaspoons deep-fried shallots (see
   Cook's Tip)
20 fresh chives, each cut into 5cm
   lengths

FOR THE DRESSING

2 tablespoons white miso paste
1–2 teaspoons toh ban jan
   (Chinese chilli bean paste)
1 tablespoon soy sauce
1 tablespoon lemon juice
2 tablespoons rice vinegar
1 tablespoon mirin
1½ teaspoons caster sugar
1 teaspoon sesame oil
2 tablespoons grape seed oil
a pinch each of salt and black pepper

Calamari squid and bamboo shoot are often used for Japanese cooking. I'm using many oriental flavours for the dressing to create an exotic salad.

SERVES 4

For the salad, first prepare the squid. Peel away the skin and wash the squid under cold running water, then pull the tentacles out. Pull the main bone out, then wash the inside again. Cut one side of the squid open and flatten it to make one sheet of calamari. Using a sharp knife, make 2mm-deep scores in a crisscross pattern on the outer side of the squid (where the skin was), then cut the squid into 5 x 2cm pieces. Set aside.

Mix all the dressing ingredients together in a large bowl and put it in the fridge.

Mix the cornflour, ½ teaspoon salt and ½ teaspoon white pepper in a small bowl. Dip each piece of squid in the cornflour mixture, making sure it is coated all over, then shake off the excess cornflour.

Heat the vegetable and sesame oils in a frying pan over a medium heat. Add the bamboo shoots with a pinch of salt and white pepper and quickly fry them for 1 minute. Turn the heat up to high and add the garlic and prepared squid. Continue to cook for a further 2 minutes.

Remove from the heat and transfer the squid and bamboo shoots to the dressing. Mix well until all are coated. Quickly finely chop the spring onions diagonally, add them to the squid mixture and toss together.

Divide the salad leaves between 4 serving plates. Spoon the squid mixture alongside the salad leaves, dividing evenly. Drizzle any remaining dressing over the salad leaves. Sprinkle the deep-fried shallots over the squid mixture, garnish with the chives and serve immediately.

COOK'S TIP
Ready-fried deep-fried shallots are available in Asian supermarkets.

TURBOT WITH MISO MUSHROOMS

FOR THE FISH

a pinch or two of salt
4 skinless turbot fillets, about
    150–200g each
2 tablespoons cornflour
2 tablespoons vegetable oil
25g butter
toasted sesame seeds and roughly
    chopped fresh coriander leaves,
    to garnish

FOR THE MISO
MUSHROOM PASTE

4 fresh shiitake mushrooms
150g fresh oyster mushrooms
100g fresh enoki mushrooms
1 teaspoon sesame oil
100g normal miso paste
2 tablespoons mirin
2 tablespoons sake
2 tablespoons mayonnaise
    (preferably Japanese mayonnaise)
1 tablespoon caster sugar

Turbot is a tasty fish in itself but it will be even tastier with this sauce. You need to be careful not to burn the sauce and not to overcook the turbot.

SERVES 4

To make the miso mushroom paste, chop all the mushrooms finely. Heat the sesame oil in a frying pan over a medium heat, add the mushrooms and cook for about 5–6 minutes or until they become soft and watery. Add the rest of miso mushroom paste ingredients and mix well. Adjust the heat to low and simmer until all the liquid has evaporated and the texture becomes like a paste rather than a sauce. Turn off the heat and keep it warm.

For the fish, lightly sprinkle the salt over the turbot fillets, then sprinkle cornflour over the salt, patting the cornflour onto the fish. Heat a large frying pan and add the vegetable oil. Cook the turbot by searing both sides in the hot oil first, then adjust the heat to medium. Cook the fish fillets for about 2 minutes on each side, then add the butter and spoon the melted butter over the fish repeatedly for about 1 minute. Take the fish out of the pan.

Preheat the grill to high. Lay the turbot fillets in a single layer in a flameproof serving dish and spread some miso mushroom paste on top of each fillet. Grill for 2 minutes or until the paste starts bubbling up.

Garnish the fish with toasted sesame seeds and chopped coriander and serve immediately.

SAKE-KASU BLACK COD

(COD MARINATED WITH SWEET FERMENTED SAKE PASTE)

OR MISO BLACK COD (COD MARINATED WITH SWEET MISO PASTE)

FOR THE BLACK COD

2 teaspoons salt
4 black cod fillets (about 150g each),
  with skin on, patted dry
vegetable oil, for greasing
4 sticks of hajikami (dark pink-
  coloured ginger stick) (optional)

FOR THE SAKE-KASU MARINADE

50g (about ¼ pack) sake-kasu (see
  Cook's Tip)
4 tablespoons hot water
1 teaspoon soy sauce
1 tablespoon mirin

FOR THE MISO MARINADE

1 tablespoon sake
2 tablespoons mirin
6 tablespoons normal miso paste
3 tablespoons caster sugar

Put all the ingredients for either the sake-kasu marinade or the miso marinade in a saucepan, bring gently to the boil, then simmer for 2 minutes, stirring to make sure all the ingredients are well combined. (If you are making miso marinade, make sure you heat and boil the sake and mirin together first for about 1 minute to evaporate the alcohol, before adding the remaining ingredients and heating them together.) Remove

I chose to include this dish in the Gourmet Dishes chapter purely because of the price of the fish and the upmarket types of restaurant that serve this dish. Black cod, simply grilled, is a mouth-watering dish.

Miso is easy to obtain but sake-kasu is a rare find. It is often used to marinade fish and is also used in soup. A hint of sake makes the flavour deep and sweet. Do try this dish once as it is an addictive taste. I have included both options for the marinade in this recipe – simply use the marinade of your choice.

SERVES 4

from the heat and leave to cool to room temperature.

Meanwhile, for the black cod, sprinkle the salt very lightly over each piece of black cod. Place on a plate and refrigerate for 1 hour, then pat dry with kitchen paper. Place the cod fillets in a shallow dish and pour over the prepared marinade. Turn the fish to coat it all over with the marinade. Cover and leave to marinate in the fridge for 2 days.

Preheat the grill to medium. Wipe the marinade completely off the fish using kitchen paper, otherwise the marinade will burn as soon as the fish is cooked (discard the marinade). Before placing the fish on the grill rack, wipe the rack with vegetable oil to prevent the fish from sticking. Place the fish fillets, skin-side down first, on the rack in the grill pan and grill for 3 minutes,

then turn them over taking care not to break the fish as the cod is very flaky and fragile. Grill for a further 3–4 minutes or until the surface edges become golden in colour and the skin becomes crispy.

If you are cooking many pieces at once, I suggest using the oven (the highest temperature) skin side up, as you won't need to turn them over.

Serve each portion with hajikami ginger sticks, if you like.

COOK'S TIPS

Hajikami is available from Japanese shops. Sake-kasu is also available from some Japanese shops (it is normally found in the freezer section).

MONKFISH AND PORCINI WITH CITRUS PONZU SOY SAUCE

FOR THE MONKFISH

2 large monkfish tails, about 400g
  each (weight with bones in)
20g dried porcini mushrooms soaked
  in 220ml hot water
1 tablespoon vegetable oil, plus
  1 teaspoon vegetable oil
30g butter, plus 1 teaspoon butter
2 tablespoons cornflour
salt and freshly ground black pepper,
  to taste
80g fresh chestnut or shimeji
  mushrooms, sliced
1 tablespoon dry or medium white
  wine
crunchy green salad vegetables,
  to serve
a little truffle oil, to serve (optional)

FOR THE CITRUS PONZU SOY
SAUCE

2½ tablespoons lemon, lime or yuzu
  (Japanese lime) juice
4 tablespoons soy sauce
2 teaspoons caster sugar

Any type of firm white fish works well for this recipe. The Japanese often use the combination of butter and soy sauce in dishes, and it works brilliantly, as this recipe demonstrates.

SERVES 4

For the monkfish, cut each monkfish tail into two fillets by removing the fillet of fish from either side of the central bone using a sharp or boning knife, taking care to leave as little flesh as possible on the bone. You will end up with four fillets in total. Discard the central bones.

Drain the soaked dried mushrooms, reserving the mushrooms and 110ml of the soaking liquid separately. Chop the mushrooms roughly. Set aside.

Heat a large frying pan over a medium heat. Add 1 tablespoon vegetable oil and 30g butter and heat until the butter has melted and mixed with the oil.

While heating the pan, season the cornflour with salt and pepper and mix well. Quickly pat the fish fillets dry with kitchen paper and dust all over with the seasoned cornflour, shaking off any excess. Add the fish to the frying pan and cook for 1 minute. Turn the fish over and turn the heat down to medium-low. Cover the fish with a piece of foil, leaving a gap for the steam to escape and cook for a further 4–5 minutes or until the fish is cooked thoroughly but is

NOT overcooked. Take the fish out of the pan as soon as it is cooked and keep it covered with the foil.

While cooking the fish, heat the remaining 1 teaspoon vegetable oil and 1 teaspoon butter in another frying pan. Add the fresh mushrooms and fry for 2 minutes or until the mushrooms are just cooked. Add the white wine, porcini and reserved porcini soaking liquid and cook for a further 1 minute over a high heat or until half of the liquid has evaporated.

Mix the ponzu soy sauce ingredients together in a small bowl, then add this to the mushrooms as soon as turned off the heat.

Place the fish on a chopping board and slice each fish fillet into 1cm-thick slices, taking care not to break the fish. Place the fish slices on serving plates alongside the crunchy green salad vegetables. Pour the mushroom mixture over the fish and sprinkle over a few drops of truffle oil, if you wish. Serve.

UNAGI EEL, DUCK LIVERS AND DAIKON TOWER

WITH RICH TERIYAKI SAUCE

½ small daikon radish
660ml dashi stock (see recipe, page 32)
1 tablespoon mirin
1 tablespoon soy sauce
salt and freshly ground black pepper,
    to taste
200g duck livers
200ml whole or semi-skimmed milk
8 baby leeks, trimmed and washed
½ tablespoon vegetable oil
400g ready-cooked unagi eel
    (1 whole eel)
2 tablespoons cornflour
20g butter
4 shallots, finely chopped
2 tablespoons brandy
110ml teriyaki sauce (see recipe, page 37)
1 tablespoon balsamic vinegar

If you fancy a little more extravagance with this recipe, use foie gras instead of duck livers. A subtleness of daikon balances up the richness unagi eel and duck livers.

SERVES 4

Cut the daikon radish diagonally into 2.5cm slices. The cut shapes should be like thick, small discs with sharp edges. Using a sharp knife, scrape off the sharp edges of each disc so that you have slices with rounder, smoother edges – this way each slice/disc holds its shape even when they are cooked until soft. (This method of preparation is called 'mentori' in Japanese.)

Heat the dashi stock in a pan with the mirin, soy sauce and a pinch of salt until boiling, then add the daikon slices, half-cover the pan and cook for about 20–30 minutes over a low heat (make sure you use a pan small enough that the daikon remains covered by the stock mixture at all times). Poke a cocktail stick into the daikon – if the cocktail stick pokes through the daikon *very* easily, then the daikon is cooked. Drain (discarding the dashi stock) and leave the daikon to cool.

Meanwhile, wash and drain the duck livers, then cut them into large bite-size pieces. Place them in a bowl, pour over the milk and leave to soak for 30 minutes. Drain the livers (discarding the milk), then wash the livers in cold water, drain again and pat them dry with kitchen paper. Set aside.

Cut each baby leek widthways into 4 even pieces. Heat the vegetable oil in a frying pan over a medium-low heat, add the leeks and fry them for about 2–3 minutes each side or until they are softened and a little caramelised, turning them occasionally. Remove the leeks to a plate and keep warm.

Preheat the grill to medium. Slice the eel into 4 equal pieces, then peel off and discard the skin. Place the eel pieces, skinned-side first, on the rack in a grill pan and grill for about 2 minutes, then turn over and grill the other side for about 1 minute. Remove the eel pieces to a plate and keep warm.

Dust the duck livers all over with the cornflour, shaking off any excess. Melt the butter in a frying pan, add the shallots and sauté for 2–3 minutes, then add the duck livers with a little salt and black pepper and cook over a medium heat for about 3 minutes. Add the brandy, immediately turn up the heat to high and flambé the livers, then cook for a further 1 minute or until all the brandy has evaporated. Remove the livers to a plate and keep warm.

In the same pan used for cooking the livers, quickly mix the teriyaki sauce and balsamic vinegar together over a low heat until the mixture becomes quite thick. The consistency should be like custard. Sieve this mixture to make a smooth sauce (the sauce should be thick enough to draw a line on a plate).

Pat the cold daikon slices dry with kitchen paper and arrange some in the centre of each serving plate. Place the eel on top, then place the duck livers on top of the eel. Drizzle some sauce over each tower. Place 8 pieces of cooked leek in a criss-cross pattern around each eel/duck tower. Serve immediately.

BEEF TATAKI WITH CREAMY SESAME SAUCE

1 large onion, thinly sliced
440ml cold water mixed with
  2 tablespoons salt
4 garlic cloves
5 tablespoons vegetable oil, plus
  3 teaspoons vegetable oil
400g beef tenderloin or fillet
  (cut lengthways into thinner pieces
  if it is too thick)
100ml soy sauce
100ml mirin
6–8 tablespoons tahini paste
2 tablespoons rice vinegar
1½ tablespoons caster sugar

Although it looks complicated and elegant, this is a very simple recipe, but it requires an understanding of the ingredients and some special skills to perfect this dish. The key is to obtain top-quality beef fillet and to cook it perfectly. It should then be served at room temperature. The garlic chips also need to be cooked until they are nice and crispy, otherwise they will spoil the dish.

SERVES 4

Put the onion slices in a bowl, pour over the salted water and leave the onions to soak for about 15 minutes. Drain, rinse well, drain again and squeeze out the excess water. Set aside.

Meanwhile, make the garlic chips. Slice the garlic cloves thinly. Heat 5 tablespoons vegetable oil in a small frying pan. Add the garlic slices and shallow-fry them slowly making sure the oil is NOT too hot. When they just start to colour, remove from the pan and leave to drain on kitchen paper (discard the oil). This should take about 5 minutes. Be careful not to cook the garlic slices until the colour is golden brown as they will continue to cook after draining on the paper. It is very important that you cook slowly as this will dehydrate the garlic and make them very crispy. Set aside.

Brush 3 teaspoons oil all over the beef. Heat a frying pan until it is hot, then add the beef and sear it on all sides as quickly as possible to seal in the juices. Reduce the heat to medium-low and continue to cook the beef until it is browned all over and it has a bouncy feel when you press it. This will take about 5–8 minutes depending on the thickness of the beef and also how much you like your beef to be cooked.

While the beef is cooking, mix the soy sauce and mirin together in a shallow dish and keep it in the fridge. Once the beef is cooked, take the dish out of the fridge and quickly dip the hot beef into the soy sauce/mirin mixture, turning the beef to make sure it is coated all over. Adding the hot beef to the chilled liquid means that the beef will stop cooking straightaway and will absorb the liquid well. Leave the beef to marinate at room temperature for about 15–30 minutes, turning it occasionally. Remove the beef to a chopping board, reserving the marinade.

Mix the reserved soy sauce/mirin marinade (used for dipping the cooked beef), tahimi paste, rice vinegar and caster sugar and mix well. Add a little cold water (if needed), mixing until the sauce becomes like thick custard in consistency.

Cut the beef into 5–7mm-thick slices and arrange on serving plates with the onions as follows – firstly, choose rectangular plates if possible, and place three small mounds (each about the size of a ping-pong ball) of onion in lines on each plate. Place the beef slices on top of each mound of onion. Pour the gomadare over the beef, taking care not to cover all the beef so that your guests can see the beautiful colour of the beef (pink inside with dark edges), as well as the sauce and onion. Sprinkle a few garlic chips over each portion and serve.

BUTA-KAKUNI

(SLOW-COOKED PORK BELLY)

2 tablespoons vegetable oil
1.2kg boneless pork belly, cut into
    7.5 x 5cm slices
200g fresh root ginger, peeled and
    cut into thick slices
2 leeks, washed, or 2 bunches spring
    onions (white part only), cut into
    chunks
1.5 litres dashi stock (see recipe on
    page 32)
110ml sake
55ml mirin
60g dark soft brown sugar
120ml soy sauce
1½ tablespoons cornflour mixed
    with 3 tablespoons cold water
1 tablespoon Japanese mustard, to
    serve
extra thinly sliced (peeled) fresh root
    ginger, to serve (optional)

This recipe creates mouth-wateringly tender and delicious pork belly! It takes a good half a day to cook but is so simple and no skill or experience is needed. The key point is to use a dark soft brown sugar – the darker the better.

SERVES 4

Heat the vegetable oil in a large, heavy-based saucepan over a high heat. Add the pork slices in two batches and sear them in the hot oil for 5–7 minutes per batch, or until browned all over.

Remove the seared pork to a plate. Quickly wash the pan, then pour plenty of hot water into the pan and add all the seared pork. Place half of the ginger slices and half of the leek chunks over the pork, then add enough extra hot water to make sure everything is covered. Bring to the boil over a high heat, then reduce the heat and simmer, uncovered, for 1½ hours, skimming the surface from time to time and topping up the hot water, if necessary. The pork needs to be covered with water at all times.

Strain the pork and discard the ginger, leeks and cooking water. Quickly rinse the pork with hot water and wash the pan. Set the pork aside.

Add the dashi stock, sake, mirin, sugar and soy sauce to the cleaned pan and stir over a high heat until all the ingredients are completely mixed. Add the pork and the remaining ginger and leeks to the pan and return to the boil. Reduce to a simmer and cook, partially covered, for 1½ to 2 hours or until the pork is very tender (you should be able to cut the pork easily with chopsticks), turning the pork occasionally.

Remove the pork to a plate, cover and keep warm. Put the pan back over a high heat, bring the liquid to the boil, then gradually stir in the combined cornflour/water mixture, stirring well until the sauce thickens. Simmer for 1 minute, stirring.

Place the pork in individual serving bowls and pour over the sauce. Serve with a little Japanese mustard on the side. You can sprinkle extra thinly sliced fresh ginger over the pork, if you wish. Simply boiled green beans is the most suitable vegetable to serve with this dish.

SEARED DUCK BREASTS

WITH SOY BALSAMIC SAUCE

200g baby leeks, trimmed and
  washed
vegetable oil, for deep-frying
15g salted butter
400ml cold water
4 boneless duck breast fillets (about
  150g each), with skin on
salt and freshly ground black pepper,
  to taste
1 garlic clove, crushed
55ml soy sauce
55ml balsamic vinegar
1 tablespoon mirin
20g unsalted butter, softened

Cut each leek into 3 and slice the top
greenish parts into very thin strips.
Heat enough vegetable oil in a small
saucepan or frying pan to give a depth
of about 2cm. Heat the oil over a
medium heat until it reaches 150°C.
Deep-fry the strips of leek (greenish
parts) in the hot oil for 1–2 minutes or
until the leeks start to crisp and become
a light golden colour. Remove from the
pan and drain on kitchen paper. Put the
salted butter and water in a separate small
saucepan and bring to the boil. Add the
remaining leeks (white parts) and cook
for 2 minutes, then drain. Set aside.

This may be a surprise, to mix soy sauce and balsamic vinegar, but it works! The saltiness of soy sauce and the sweet acidity of the balsamic vinegar go well with the gamey flavour of the duck. By cooking duck this way, the skin becomes crispy and the flesh stays succulent.

SERVES 4

Pluck any little hairs off the duck skin, then trim off the excess skin making sure you leave enough skin on to completely cover one side of each breast. Make three incisions in the skin on each breast, taking care not to cut through to the flesh.

Heat a large, heavy-based pan without any oil, then place the duck breasts into the pan, skin-side down. Season the duck with salt and pepper. Cover the pan with a lid but leave a small gap for the steam to escape and cook for 5 minutes over a medium-low heat. When the duck starts to release its fat into the pan, add the garlic and shake the pan gently.

Turn the duck fillets over and cook for 2 minutes. Season the skin of the duck with salt and pepper. Turn the duck fillets again so they are skin-side down and cook for a further 3–5 minutes, depending on how you like your duck cooked. Always cook with the lid on but leaving a small gap to allow steam to escape, otherwise the skin will become soggy.

While the duck is cooking, mix the soy sauce, balsamic vinegar and mirin together in a small saucepan. Bring to the boil, then cook over a fairly high heat until the mixture has reduced by about a third and becomes thickened. Add the unsalted butter just before turning off the heat and shake the pan to melt the butter. Keep warm.

Take the duck fillets out of the pan and leave them to rest on a chopping board, covered with foil, for 1–2 minutes.

While the duck is resting, drain most of the duck fat from the pan, then quickly fry the boiled leeks in the remaining fat for 2–3 minutes.

Slice each duck breast into thin slices and arrange them on 4 individual plates. Place the boiled, fried leeks alongside and drizzle the sauce over. Finally, scatter the deep-fried leeks over the duck and serve immediately.

COOK'S TIP
Instead of deep-frying the leeks for the garnish, you can simply shallow-fry them in a little hot vegetable oil until they are light golden in colour, if you prefer.

LAMB WITH MISO, BLUE CHEESE AND APPLE SAUCE

FOR THE LAMB AND BEANS
4 lamb fillets, about 200g each
250g frozen edamame beans
    (young soya beans)
2 teaspoons salt
2 tablespoons vegetable oil

FOR THE MARINADE

3 tablespoons normal miso paste
3 tablespoons caster sugar
3 tablespoons mirin
3 tablespoons vegetable oil

FOR THE SWEET MISO SAUCE

2 tablespoons white miso paste
1 tablespoon blue cheese, such as
    Roquefort
2 tablespoons mirin
1 tablespoon caster sugar
3 tablespoons fresh unsweetened
    apple juice
1 teaspoon grated (peeled) fresh root
    ginger

This dish is a great example of a fusion dish. Miso is an authentic Japanese ingredient which is combined with a non-traditional Japanese food, blue cheese, to create an interesting flavour combination. Apple juice adds both sharpness and sweetness to the salty, fermented-flavoured sauce.

SERVES 4

For the lamb, slice off all the sinew from the lamb fillets, otherwise the sinew will be tighten up when cooked and the fillets will become rumps.

Mix all the ingredients for the marinade together in a bowl, stirring until all the sugar has dissolved and no lumps of miso paste remain. Place the lamb fillets in a shallow dish and pour over the marinade mixture, turning the lamb over to make sure it is completely coated. Cover and leave to marinade in the fridge for between 6–12 hours.

Cook the edamame beans. Bring a large pan of water to the boil and add the salt. Add the beans, bring back to the boil and cook for 3 minutes. Rinse under cold water, then drain well and remove the beans from the pods (discard the pods). Set the beans aside.

Wipe the marinade off the meat using kitchen paper. Heat the vegetable oil in a frying pan over a medium heat, add the lamb fillets and sear them all over, turning frequently. Turn the heat down to medium-low and continue to cook

the lamb fillets for a further 4–5 minutes or until they are cooked to your liking, turning occasionally.

While the lamb is cooking, put all the sweet miso sauce ingredients, except the ginger, into a small saucepan. Bring to the boil and simmer for about 3–4 minutes or until well mixed and the sauce becomes slightly syrupy in consistency, stirring occasionally. Stir in the ginger and sieve through the sauce just before sering.

Remove the meat from the pan to a chopping board and leave it to rest for 1–2 minutes. Slice each fillet into 1cm-thick slices and arrange the lamb slices on individual serving plates. Pour the sauce over the lamb and sprinkle the beans around the lamb. Serve immediately.

SEA BREAM RICE

320g short-grain white rice
1 small sheet of dried sea kelp
   (konbu or kombu) (about 10g)
440ml cold water
10cm long piece fresh root ginger
2 large sea bream fillets (about 150g
   each), with skin on
1 teaspoon good-quality sea salt
2 tablespoons soy sauce, plus extra
   for serving
1 tablespoon sake
1 tablespoon mirin

Sea Bream is often used for special occasions or celebrations in Japan. Sea bream is called 'tai' in Japanese and 'medetai' is the Japanese word for 'Let's celebrate!' The method of cooking this dish is very simple, therefore it is extremely important to use the best quality fish and get the timings just right.

SERVES 4

Wash and drain the rice, then place it in a flameproof casserole dish with the sea kelp and cover with the water. Leave to soak for 1 hour.

Peel the ginger and slice half of the ginger (slicing against the fibres) into thin slices; cut the remaining ginger into thin, needle-like sticks. Set aside.

Wash the fish thoroughly, making sure all the bones are removed. Make a few scores in the skin-side of the fish, then sprinkle a little sea salt over the fish.

Place a few sticks of ginger on top of the rice and sea kelp in the casserole dish, place the fish on top, then place a few more sticks of ginger on top of the fish. Mix the soy sauce, sake and mirin together in a small bowl, then pour this mixture into the casserole dish.

Cover the casserole and start cooking the rice over the highest heat until it comes to the boil (it will take longer to reach boiling point in a casserole dish than in a normal saucepan). Once it reaches the boil, turn the heat down to the lowest setting and simmer for about 15 minutes, keeping the lid on at all times.

Turn the heat off, then leave the casserole to stand, with the lid on, for about 10–12 minutes, to finish cooking the rice. (If you are using an electric hob, remove the casserole away from the hob and leave it to stand.) Once the rice is cooked, remove the lid, carefully remove the sea kelp and ginger, then put the lid back on.

Serve the cooked rice and fish with thinly sliced ginger and extra soy sauce as condiments on the side. Take the casserole to the table and remove the lid in front of your guests, then carefully serve the rice to them. Alternatively, you can serve the rice in individual serving bowls and take these to your guests at the table.

SALMON TARTARE ON SUSHI RICE

WITH WASABI MAYONNAISE

FOR THE SALMON

2 tablespoons ikura (salmon fish roe)
½ teaspoon soy sauce
½ teaspoon mirin
20 seedless white grapes
150g fresh sashimi-quality salmon
   fillet (skinless)
1 ripe avocado, halved, stoned and
   peeled
2–3 teaspoons lemon juice
1 teaspoon finely grated lemon zest
1 tablespoon finely chopped fresh
   parsley
800g cooked sushi rice (see recipe on
   page 35) (serve at room
   temperature)
4 fresh parsley sprigs, to garnish

FOR THE WASABI MAYONNAISE

3 large egg yolks
½ teaspoon salt
1 tablespoon lemon juice
3 tablespoons rice vinegar
2 tablespoons soy sauce
2 tablespoons Dijon mustard
about 500ml vegetable oil
4 teaspoons wasabi paste

This is a truly vibrant and beautiful dish that has a real 'wow factor'. The orange from the salmon roe, the green from the avocado and grapes, the yellow from the mayonnaise...springtime has arrived on the table!

SERVES 4

For the salmon, gently mix the salmon roe, soy sauce and mirin together in a small bowl and set aside in the fridge for 30 minutes.

Meanwhile, peel the grapes and slice them in half (this is time-consuming, but it needs to be done, otherwise the texture will be spoiled). Cut the salmon and avocado into 1cm dice. Toss the avocado pieces in the lemon juice to stop them discolouring. Set aside.

For the wasabi mayonnaise, place all the ingredients, except the vegetable oil and wasabi paste, in a bowl and mix together. Gradually and very slowly add the oil to the mixture, whisking it all the time. Stop adding oil and whisking when the consistency becomes like runny (pourable) mayonnaise. Add the wasabi paste, little by little, tasting the mixture as you go until the flavour is to your liking.

Combine the salmon, avocado, lemon zest, chopped parsley and two-thirds of the grapes with the sushi rice in a large bowl and mix gently.

Divide the rice mixture between 4 serving plates, shaping each portion into a small pointed mountain on each plate. Pour the wasabi mayonnaise (to your taste) over the rice and sprinkle the rest of grapes and the ikura mixture over the top. Be careful not to cover all the rice with the mayonnaise, or you will not be able to see the beautiful orange and green colours from the other ingredients. Garnish each portion with a sprig of parsley and serve.

COOK'S TIPS
Ikura (salmon fish roe) is available from Japanese fishmongers. Any leftover mayonnaise can be kept in an airtight container in the fridge for up to 3 days.

MENTAIKO

(CHILLI-SPICED COD ROE AND LUMPFISH CAVIAR SPAGHETTI)

320g dried spaghetti or capellini
  (angel hair pasta)
1 tablespoon salt
100g mentaiko (chilli-spiced cod roe)
4 tablespoons Japanese mayonnaise
1 egg yolk
2–3 tablespoons soy sauce
2 tablespoons mirin
2 tablespoons olive oil
30g butter
seven-spice chilli powder, to taste
3 tablespoons lumpfish caviar
2 nori sheets (each about 19cm
  square), broken into small pieces

Mentaiko is a very popular ingredient in Japan. It is often simply eaten with rice as it has a strong, fishy flavour. Mentaiko spaghetti was created about 40–50 years ago when people started to eat pasta regularly. I have created this Western version of the original Japanese dish, with a more appealing flavour for Westerners, so I hope you enjoy it.

SERVES 4

Cook the pasta in a large pan of boiling water with the salt added, according to the packet directions or until al dente.

Meanwhile, squeeze the little mentaiko roes out of their skins into a large bowl (later, all the ingredients will be mixed in this bowl, so choose a large one!). Add the mayonnaise, egg yolk, soy sauce and mirin to the bowl and mix well. Set aside.

Heat the olive oil and butter together in a large frying pan or a wok. Drain the spaghetti well, then quickly transfer it to the frying pan. Toss the spaghetti in the melted butter and oil mixture over a medium-high heat for 1 minute. Season the pasta with the seven-spice chilli powder.

Transfer the spaghetti into the mentaiko mixture and quickly toss everything together, making sure all the ingredients are mixed together well. Add the lumpfish caviar and mix very gently.

Place the spaghetti like a small mountain in the centre of each serving bowl or plate, dividing it evenly, then sprinkle small pieces of nori over the top of the pasta and serve.

CHA-SOBA NOODLE AND CALAMARI WITH YAKUMI SAUCE

FOR THE NOODLES

200g dried cha-soba noodle or
   normal soba noodle
2 tablespoons vegetable oil
100g fresh squid or calamari (main
   bone removed)
100g minced pork
1 yellow pepper, deseeded and thinly
   sliced
1 fresh red chilli, deseeded and thinly
   sliced
½ tablespoon thinly sliced (peeled)
   fresh root ginger
a pinch of salt and white pepper
½ cucumber, finely chopped
2 tablespoons thinly sliced spring
   onions
4 tablespoons roughly chopped fresh
   coriander

FOR THE YAKUMI SAUCE

125ml dashi stock (see recipe on
   page 32)
2 tablespoons soy sauce
1 tablespoon fish sauce (nam pla)
½ teaspoon sesame oil
1 tablespoon mirin
1 teaspoon grated (peeled) fresh root
   ginger
½ teaspoon dark soft brown sugar

'Cha' as the word for tea in Japanese. 'Cha-Soba' is a green tea-flavoured soba noodle. Admittedly, it is not so much the flavour than the colour that is used to create this colourful dish.

SERVES 4

Prepare the noodles. Cook the soba noodle in a large pan of boiling water for about 4–5 minutes until cooked or slightly al dente. Rinse under running cold water to remove the starch, drain, then toss with 1 tablespoon vegetable oil. Set aside.

Meanwhile, combine all the ingredients for the yakumi sauce in a small bowl, stirring well to make sure all the sugar is completely dissolved. Set aside.

Peel away the skin and wash the squid under cold running water. Cut one side of the squid open and flatten it out. Using a sharp knife, make 2mm-deep scores in a crisscross pattern on the outer side of the squid (where the skin was), then cut the squid into 5 x 1cm strips. If you are using the tentacles, there is no need to take the skin off but cut and separate them into reasonable bite-size pieces.

Heat the remaining oil in a saucepan, add the minced pork, yellow pepper, red chilli, ginger and salt and white pepper. Cook for about 2–3 minutes or until the pork is browned all over, stirring regularly. Add the squid and cucumber and cook for a further 1 minute or until the squid is just cooked.

Add the yakumi sauce to the pan and turn the heat up to high. Once the sauce is boiling, add the noodles and spring onions and toss everything together while quickly heating up the noodles.

Once the noodles are thoroughly heated, transfer the mixture to individual serving bowls. Garnish each portion with a sprinkling of chopped coriander and serve.

TOFU DENGAKU-TRIPLE COLOUR

FOR THE TOFU

600g firm tofu
vegetable oil, for brushing

FOR THE WHITE DENGAKU MISO

4 tablespoons white miso paste
1 tablespoon mirin
1 tablespoon caster sugar
2 tablespoons cold water
2 egg yolks

FOR THE DARK DENGAKU MISO

1 tablespoon freshly ground black
   sesame seeds
1 tablespoon white dengaku miso
   (from above)
½ teaspoon cold water, if necessary

FOR THE GREEN
DENGAKU MISO

2 teaspoons shiso leaves, watercress
   or fresh coriander, freshly ground
   (ground using a pestle and mortar)
1 tablespoon white dengaku miso
   (from above)

This is one of the most traditional and popular dishes in Japan. By using these simple ingredients, you can create a dish with a subtle and sophisticated flavour. It's like a little art presented on each plate.

SERVES 4

Prepare the tofu. Wrap the tofu in kitchen paper, place it on a chopping board and place a heavy chopping board on top, to squeeze the water out. Leave it for a couple of hours. Alternatively, cook the tofu in a pan of boiling water for 2–3 minutes, then drain well. Slice the tofu in half, then leave it to cool – this way the water from the tofu naturally drains out.

To make the white dengaku miso, place all the ingredients, except the egg yolks, in a bowl and mix together well. Transfer the mixture to a small saucepan and cook over a low heat, stirring all the time. Cook for about 2–3 minutes or until the mixture becomes quite sticky. Add the egg yolks, then simmer for a further 1 minute, stirring very quickly and mixing well. Remove from the heat and leave to cool.

To make the dark dengaku miso, simply mix the ground sesame seeds into the cooled white dengaku miso. As the ground seeds are dry, the texture may be too thick, so you may need to stir in a little water if that is the case.

To make the green dengaku miso, simply mix the chosen ground green herb into the cooled white dengaku miso, mixing thoroughly until the colour becomes green.

Cut the tofu into 12 even slices. Preheat the grill to medium. Brush vegetable oil all over each slice of tofu. Place the tofu slices on the rack in a grill pan and grill for about 3–4 minutes on each side, turning once.

Spread the dengaku miso mixtures over the top of the tofu slices (spread each batch of miso mixture over 4 slices of tofu) – each person should end up with 3 slices of tofu, each with a different-coloured miso topping. Return to the grill and grill for a further 2 minutes or until the dengaku miso starts to bubble up and becomes lightly charred. Serve immediately.

GANMODOKI TOFU

(TOFU PATTIES) WITH GINGER CLEAR BROTH

FOR THE TOFU PATTIES

20g dried hijiki seasweed or dried
  shiitake mushrooms
300ml warm water
1/2 teaspoon caster sugar
400g firm tofu
110ml dashi stock (see recipe on
  page 32)
1 teaspoon soy sauce
1 teaspoon mirin
1 carrot, cut into short, thin
  matchsticks
1/2 egg white
a pinch of salt
2 tablespoons cornflour, plus 120g
  cornflour for dusting
vegetable oil (at least 1 litre), for
  deep-frying

FOR THE FRESH GINGER BROTH

440ml dashi stock
2 tablespoons soy sauce
2 tablespoons mirin
1 tablespoon sake
a pinch of salt
1 1/2 tablespoons cornflour
4 tablespoons cold water
1 tablespoon grated (peeled) fresh
  root ginger

This dish is one skill level up from Agedashi Tofu (in the beginner's section). It has more texture but you can add even more, if you like. Try using minced chicken or more vegetables.

SERVES 4

Prepare the tofu patties. Put the mushrooms in a bowl and pour over the combined warm water and sugar. Leave to soak for 1 hour or until soft. Drain well (discarding the soaking liquid). Finely chop the soaked mushrooms.

Wrap the tofu in a large muslin cloth or kitchen paper and squeeze out as much water as possible.

Put the dashi stock in a saucepan with the soy sauce, mirin, carrot sticks and hijiki seaweed or chopped mushrooms. Bring gently to the boil and cook for 3 minutes, then drain well, discarding the stock mixture but reserving the carrots and mushrooms.

In a large bowl, combine the tofu, carrot sticks, seaweed or mushrooms (making sure excess moisture squeezed out), egg white and a pinch of salt, mixing thoroughly. Check the consistency of the tofu mixture to see if it is firm enough to make balls. If it is too soft, add enough of the 2 tablespoons cornflour, a little by little, until you have the correct consistency. Divide the mixture into 8 equal portions, then shape each

portion into a 5cm round flattened patty.

Heat the vegetable oil in a deep, heavy-based saucepan or a wok over a medium heat until it reaches 170°C. (To check that the temperature of the oil is hot enough, see method of Tonkatsu recipe on page 38.)

Lightly dust the tofu patties all over with the remaining cornflour, shaking off any excess. Deep-fry the patties in the hot oil over a medium-high heat for 2–3 minutes or until light golden colour all over.

Meanwhile, put all the ginger broth ingredients, except the cornflour, cold water and fresh ginger, in a separate saucepan and bring to the boil. Mix the cornflour and cold water in a small cup until smooth, then pour this into the boiling broth and mix thoroughly until the broth is thickened and smooth. Simmer for 1 minute, stirring, then remove from the heat.

Place 2 tofu patties in each of 4 individual serving bowls and pour over the thickened broth. Serve with the grated ginger on the side.

TOFU STEAK WITH MUSHROOM TOPPING

600g firm tofu
250–300g mixed fresh shiitake and
　enoki mushrooms
6 spring onions
3 tablespoons cornflour
a pinch of salt
a pinch of white pepper
a pinch of sansho pepper
1½ tablespoons vegetable or
　sunflower oil
1 teaspoon sesame oil
25g butter
1 garlic clove, thinly sliced
2 teaspoons grated (peeled) fresh
　root ginger
70g streaky bacon, cut into 1cm
　strips
2 tablespoons soy sauce
2 tablespoons mirin
2 tablespoons bonito flakes

For those who are not so keen on the flavour of tofu, you might like to try this dish. The interesting combination of the mushroom topping and the crispy, subtle tofu steaks, creates an appealing dish. You may also like to try this dish with white fish instead of tofu.

SERVES 4

Wrap the tofu in a couple of layers of kitchen paper, place on a chopping board, then place a heavy chopping board on top. Leave it for 1–2 hours to squeeze out as much water as possible, but be careful not to break the tofu.

Cut the mushrooms into small bite-size pieces and finely chop the spring onions, keeping the white and green parts separate. Set aside.

Pat the tofu dry and cut the block in half horizontally, so you have 2 thinner slices of tofu. Cut each of these slices into quarters, so you then have 8 even slices in total. Combine the cornflour and seasonings, then dust the tofu all over with the seasoned cornflour, patting the cornflour onto the tofu.

Heat 1 tablespoon vegetable oil and the sesame oil in a large frying pan until hot. Carefully slide the tofu slices into the pan and cook for about 3 minutes on each side or until the tofu becomes light golden in colour, carefully turning over once.

While the tofu is cooking, heat the butter and remaining vegetable oil in a separate frying pan over a medium-high heat. Add the garlic, ginger, bacon, white parts of the spring onions and the mushrooms and cook for 3–4 minutes or until the mushrooms are softened and the bacon is thoroughly cooked, stirring occasionally. Add the soy sauce and mirin. Turn the heat up to high and stir until any liquid is almost evaporated, then remove from the heat.

Place the tofu slices on 4 individual serving plates and spoon the mushroom mixture over the tofu. Sprinkle with the chopped green parts of the spring onions and the bonito flakes. Serve immediately.

TOFU CHAWANMUSHI

(SAVOURY EGG CUSTARD) WITH UNAGI EEL AND PRAWNS

FOR THE UNAGI EEL MIXTURE

150g ready-cooked unagi eel
(cooked in teriyaki sauce)
100g fresh spinach leaves, rinsed
2 pinches of salt
10 pods of fresh (or frozen, if fresh
not available) edamame beans
(young soya beans)
80g small fresh peeled prawns
a few fresh watercress sprigs or
finely snipped fresh chives, to
garnish

FOR THE EGG CUSTARD MIXTURE

200g silken tofu
3 eggs, beaten
330ml dashi stock (see recipe on
page 32), at room temperature
1 tablespoon soy sauce
2 teaspoons mirin
1/2 teaspoon salt

As 'Chawanmushi' is regarded as 'a strange savoury dish resembling the texture of crème caramel', for the Western pallet. This dish might be a brave dish for you to try! All I can say is please try it, then you will know why I'm including
it here.

SERVES 4

Prepare the eel. Preheat the grill to medium-high. Remove the eel from the packet and place it, skin-side down, on the rack in a grill pan. Grill for 2 minutes, then remove it from the heat. Let it cool slightly, then remove and discard the skin and slice the eel into small bite-size pieces, taking care not to break the eel. If the eel is still hot, it's more difficult to slice, so wait until it has cooled down. Set aside.

Quickly blanch the spinach leaves in a pan of boiling water with a pinch of salt added for 15 seconds, then drain under cold running water for 10 seconds. Drain well and squeeze out the water. Break up the tightly squeezed spinach by flaking it into pieces using your fingers, or chop the spinach, if necessary. Cook the edamame beans in the same pan of freshly boiled water with a pinch of salt added for 5 minutes, then drain. Remove the beans from their pods (discard the pods). Set the spinach and beans aside.

For the egg custard mixture, wrap the tofu in a piece of muslin cloth or kitchen paper and squeeze out as much water as possible. Break up the tofu with a whisk in a bowl. In a separate bowl, mix the eggs, dashi stock, soy sauce, mirin and salt together. Sieve the egg mixture into the bowl containing the tofu and mix until well combined.

Place the spinach, edamame beans, prawns and three-quarters of the unagi eel into a large bowl or individual chawanmushi cups (dividing evenly if serving individual portions). Pour the tofu and egg mixture into the bowl or the cups.

Place the bowl or cups in a steamer and set the steamer over a medium-high heat at first. Wrap the lid of the steamer with a cloth and tie up the top to secure the cloth with a rubber band so that the condensation will not drip over the tofu mixture. (The condensation drips will change the texture of the custard mixture and this must be avoided.) Steam for 2 minutes, then reduce the heat to medium-low.

Steam gently for a further 18–20 minutes for the large bowl and 13–15 minutes for the small cups – cooking time will really depend on the size/depth of the bowl(s) used. If they are cooked, when you insert a toothpick into the centre of the egg custard, a little clear liquid will come out onto the surface; if they are not cooked, cloudy egg liquid will appear on the surface, so you will need to cook them for a little longer. Remove the bowl(s) from the steamer and leave to set for 2 minutes.

Finally, top the steamed egg custard(s) with the remaining unagi eel – if you are using the individual cups, place about 2 pieces of eel on top of each portion; if you have made one large egg custard, scatter the eel pieces decoratively over the top of the whole dish. Garnish with watercress sprigs or snipped chives and serve immediately.

SUSHI

187 STANDARD PREPARATION FOR MAKING SUSHI / SUGGESTED TOPPINGS AND FILLINGS
190 SUSHI RECIPES

STANDARD PREPARATION FOR MAKING SUSHI

Make the sushi rice. The quantity of cooked sushi rice needed is about 1 cup of rice per person, which is about 150g per person. Cooked sushi rice is always served at room temperature (unless specified otherwise in a recipe).

Prepare all the fillings and toppings accordingly. For example, prepare long thin sticks for the rolls; small thin slices for the hand-moulded sushi; thin wide pieces for the compressed sushi.

Alternatively, soft, paste-like mixtures (such as salmon or tuna mayonnaise, salmon mousse, dressed crab, houmus, etc) can be used for any type and shape of sushi.

A bowl of cold water is needed whenever handling sushi rice as it is very sticky. Wetting your hands helps to keep rice from sticking to your hands to a minimum.

Make sure you have all the necessary utensils to make the sushi, depending on which types of sushi you are preparing.

Buy and use pickled ginger and wasabi paste as a garnish.

SUGGESTED TOPPINGS AND FILLINGS

RAW INGREDIENTS

Fish – many fish can be eaten raw, but not all. Consult with your fishmonger when choosing the fish for sushi and also when making nigiri as you need a particular variety of fish for this recipe. The ideal types of fish for the rolls are tuna and salmon, due to their colour and popularity.

Fish roe – salmon roe (ikura), flying fish roe (tobiko), cod roe (tarako) and so on, are all suitable for sushi.

Shellfish – scallops, sea urchin, prawns, cuttlefish, crabmeat, squid, boiled octopus and so on, are all suitable for sushi.

COOKED INGREDIENTS

Fish – grilled eel, cooked peeled prawns, smoked mackerel, smoked salmon, canned salmon or tuna with mayonnaise, good-quality crabsticks, etc, are all suitable for sushi.

Meat – seared beef or duck, sliced thinly, are both ideal for nigiri. Teriyaki or steamed chicken (see recipes on pages 75 and 113) can be used for sushi.

Vegetables – many vegetables can be used for sushi, including seeded cucumber, avocado, daikon pickles (takuan), roasted red and yellow peppers, and so on.

Vegetarian options – smoked or deep-fried tofu, cooked mushrooms, houmus, etc, are all suitable for sushi.

Tamago-Yaki (see recipe on page 56) is also suitable for sushi.

Sushi: Japan's national dish and one you can enjoy cheaply and easily at home if you follow the step-by-step recipes over the following pages of this chapter.

SABA OSHI-ZUSHI

(MACKEREL COMPRESSED SUSHI)

1 teaspoon salt
1 large fresh mackerel fillet (about 200g), with skin on
110–165ml sushi vinegar (see recipe on page 35)
600g cooked sushi rice (see recipe on page 35)
2 tablespoons pickled ginger, drained and chopped

Oshi-Zushi is the very first sushi to have been created. Originally, this was a way of preserving fish and this is why, traditionally, pickled fish is used for this recipe. The most popular fish used for this dish is mackerel, but you may like to try sea bass or sea bream instead, for a more subtle flavour.

SERVES 4

Pickle the mackerel first. Sprinkle the salt lightly all over the very fresh fillet of mackerel on a plate and leave it for 10–15 minutes. Pat the mackerel dry with kitchen paper. Put the mackerel in a shallow dish and pour over the sushi vinegar (to a depth of about 1cm, so that it almost covers the fish). Cover the dish with cling film and leave to marinate in the fridge, preferably overnight or for at least half a day, turning the fish a few times to make sure the fish is evenly marinated all over.

Once the mackerel is pickled, remove it from the vinegar (discard the vinegar), then carefully and slowly peel off the thin film covering the skin of the mackerel, taking care not to peel off the pattern of the skin. (If you cook mackerel, this film dissolves, but if you marinate it, this film becomes thicker and rubbery in texture, which is not pleasant to eat.)

Line the inside of a wooden compressed sushi mould or a rectangular container with a lid (dimensions about 20 x 10 x 5cm) with cling film, allowing the cling film to drape over the top of the mould. Fill the mould with the sushi rice, spreading and pressing it down evenly.

Spoon the pickled ginger evenly over the rice and lay the whole pickled mackerel on top.

Wrap the whole sushi in cling film, covering it completely. Cover with the lid (the lid should fit inside the mould/container) and place a weight, such as a few heavy books, on top. Leave it in a cool place for at least 2 hours to compress it properly and to allow the rice to absorb the flavour from the pickled mackerel and ginger.

Remove the whole compressed block of sushi (still wrapped in cling film) from the mould. Remove and discard the cling film, then cut the block into 2cm-thick slices. Serve.

OSHI-ZUSHI (COMPRESSED), FASHION SANDWICH

SMOKED SALMON OSHI-ZUSHI

600g cooked sushi rice (see recipe on page 35)
100g canned red salmon (drained weight), drained and any bones removed
1 tablespoon finely chopped spring onions
2 tablespoon mayonnaise (preferably Japanese mayonnaise)
1 teaspoon soy sauce
2 large slices smoked salmon (about 100g)
fresh coriander sprigs, shiso leaves, fresh dill sprigs, lumpfish caviar or capers, to garnish (optional)

The two Oshi-Zushi (smoked salmon and vegetarian) recipes introduced here are the modern versions of Oshi-Zushi. As pickled fish is an acquired taste, I am including these two different versions to suit all tastes, but by all means try whatever toppings/fillings you fancy. These are perfect for canapés.

SERVES 4

Line the inside of a wooden compressed sushi mould or rectangular container with a lid (dimensions about 20 x 10 x 5cm) with cling film, allowing the cling film to drape over the top of the mould. Fill the mould with half of the sushi rice, spreading and pressing it down evenly.

Combine the canned salmon, spring onions, mayonnaise and soy sauce in a bowl, mixing well, then spread this mixture evenly over the rice.

Spread the remaining sushi rice over the top of the canned salmon mixture, pressing it down evenly. Lay the smoked salmon slices on top.

Wrap the whole sushi in cling film, covering it completely. Cover with the lid (the lid should fit inside the mould/container) and place a weight, such as a few heavy books, on top. Leave it in a cool place for at least 2 hours to compress it properly and to allow the rice to absorb the flavour from the filling and topping.

Remove the whole compressed block of sushi (still wrapped in cling film) from the mould. Remove and discard the cling film, then cut the block into 2.5cm cubes or large bite-size pieces. Decorate each piece with the herbs, lumpfish caviar or capers, if you wish. Serve.

VEGETARIAN OSHI-ZUSHI

Make as for Smoked Salmon Oshi-Zushi, but replace the canned salmon mixture with a combination of 3 tablespoons houmus and 2 tablespoons snipped fresh chives. Omit the smoked salmon. Slice $1/2$ roasted red pepper and $1/2$ roasted yellow pepper into 1-cm-thick slices. Lay the pepper slices, alternately and diagonally, across the top of the top layer of rice. Cover, compress, garnish (with fresh herbs) and serve as for Smoked Salmon Oshi-Zushi.

HOSO MAKI-ZUSHI

(THIN ROLLS)

TUNA HOSO MAKI-ZUSHI

2 nori sheets (each about 19cm
   square), each cut in half
300g cooked sushi rice (see recipe on
   page 35)
wasabi paste, to taste (optional)
120g fresh sashimi-quality tuna, cut
   into thin strips

This is the most familiar version of sushi outside of Japan. Traditionally raw fish is used for the filling, but nowadays, many different fillings are used. Why not try using a selection of pickled or cooked vegetables instead of the fish, for a change?

MAKES 4 ROLLS

For each roll, place a bamboo sushi mat on the table. Place one nori sheet half on the mat horizontally, with the rough side up, leaving a margin of about 2.5cm on the side of the mat closest to you. Dip your hands in cold water, shake off the excess, then scoop up a quarter of the sushi rice. Spread the sushi rice over the nori sheet to cover it evenly, leaving a 1cm margin on the side farthest from you. Spread the rice so the surface is relatively smooth but do not press down on it too hard.

Spread a little wasabi paste over the rice, if you like, then arrange a quarter of the tuna strips horizontally across the centre of the rice. Cut off the excess fish if the strips are too long, but always allow the filling to go slightly over the edge of the nori sheet.

Using both hands, pick up the side of the sushi mat closest to you with your index fingers and thumbs. Carefully roll up the nori sheet (using the bamboo mat as a guide to do this), enclosing the filling inside the nori sheet as you roll, rolling away from you towards the far side. When rolled up, hold the sushi mat around the roll with both hands and squeeze and pat it gently to firm and shape the roll.

Leave the nori roll, seam-side down, on a chopping board for at least 3 minutes, so that the seam in the nori will become glued naturally. Do not try to glue the nori with water or it will dissolve and lose its shape. During this standing time, the nori will shrink slightly, therefore it's important to rest it for a few minutes before cutting.

Repeat with the remaining nori sheet halves, sushi rice, wasabi paste and tuna, to make a total of 4 rolls. Cut each roll into 6 slices before serving.

UNA-KYU HOSO MAKI-ZUSHI

(UNAGI EEL AND CUCUMBER ROLLS)

2 nori sheets (each about 19cm
square), each cut in half
300g cooked sushi rice (see recipe on
page 35)
wasabi paste, to taste (optional)
100g grilled eel (see Tofu
Chawanmushi recipe on page
182), cooled and thinly sliced
½ small cucumber, cut into
matchsticks

Make and assemble as for Tuna Hoso
Maki-Zushi, but replace the tuna with
the eel and cucumber.

CALIFORNIAN ROLL, URA MAKI-ZUSHI

(INSIDE-OUT ROLLS)

2 nori sheets (each about 19cm square), each cut in half
450g cooked sushi rice (see recipe on page 35)
60g flying fish roe (tobiko)
4 tablespoons black sesame seeds
wasabi paste, to taste (optional)
1 avocado, peeled, stoned and cut into segments
100–120g cooked peeled prawns, good-quality crabsticks (flaked or chopped) or salmon mayonnaise (see Cook's Tips)
½ cucumber, cut into matchsticks

This is a slightly more complicated version of sushi rolls that was created in the 1960s. Not only can you enjoy extra flavour with this sushi but it is also very pretty to look at. You just need some practice to master the technique of making it.

MAKES 4 ROLLS

For each roll, place a bamboo sushi mat on the table. Place one nori sheet half on the mat horizontally. Dip your hands in cold water, shake off the excess, then scoop up a quarter of the sushi rice. Spread the sushi rice over the nori sheet to cover it evenly. Spread the rice so the surface is relatively smooth but do not press down on it too hard.

Sprinkle 15g of the flying fish roe, then 1 tablespoon of the black sesame seeds evenly over the rice. Cover the entire surface with cling film. Place another bamboo sushi mat over the top and press it down lightly, then turn it all over. Now you have the original sushi mat on the top, so remove this mat.

Spread a little wasabi paste over the nori sheet, if you like, then lay the fillings (first a quarter of the avocado, then a quarter of the seafood, and finally a quarter of the cucumber) horizontally across the centre of the nori sheet, always allowing the filling to go slightly over the edge of the nori sheet.

Using both hands, pick up the side of the sushi mat and cling film closest to you with your index fingers and thumbs. Carefully roll up the nori sheet (using the bamboo mat and cling film as a guide to do this), enclosing the filling (but not the cling film) inside the nori sheet as you roll, rolling away from you towards the far side. Try to roll as tightly as possible, otherwise the fillings can quite easily come out (as the nori is enclosing and holding the fillings together, not the sticky rice). When rolled up, hold the sushi mat around the roll with both hands and squeeze and pat it gently to firm and shape the roll.

Leave the nori roll, seam-side down, on a chopping board for at least 3 minutes, so that the seam in the nori will become glued naturally. During this standing time, the nori will shrink slightly, therefore it's important to rest it for a few minutes before cutting.

Repeat with the remaining ingredients to make a total of 4 rolls. Cut each roll into 8 slices before serving.

COOK'S TIPS
Flying fish roe (tobiko) is available from Japanese fishmongers. Salmon mayonnaise is simply canned (drained) salmon, flaked and combined with mayonnaise (preferably Japanese mayonnaise). Canned tuna can be used to make tuna mayonnaise in the same way and this can also be used for this recipe.

NSIDE-OUT ROLLS:
THE STEP-BY-STEP BASICS

1

2

Fan the sushi rice.

and 3. Lay the fillings onto the
nori sheet.

Pick up the mat with both
hands, ready to roll.

Roll away from the body,
keeping the mat held tightly.

After firming and shaping the
roll and leaving to stand, cut the
sushi into neat slices.

3

4

5

6

GOURMET URA MAKI-ZUSHI

2 avocados (not too ripe)

2 nori sheets (each about 19cm square), each cut in half

450g cooked sushi rice (see recipe on page 35)

3 tablespoons mayonnaise (preferably Japanese mayonnaise)

1 teaspoon wasabi paste (optional)

60g flying fish roe (tobiko)

a handful of shredded iceberg lettuce

8 medium tempura prawns (see recipe on page 63), cooked and left to cool to room temperature

These sushi rolls require the most skill to make them, hence, I would recommend that you first try making the normal rolls before you try making these. Leftover tempura prawns or tempura vegetables from the night before can be used for this recipe. Make sure the avocado is not too ripe or soft, otherwise it will become squashed, but also don't choose one that is too hard or unripe!

MAKES 4 ROLLS

Cut each avocado lengthways into quarters, remove the stone and peel off the skin. Slice each quarter of avocado into very thin slices – each quarter should make 6–7 thin slices. Set aside.

For each roll, place a bamboo sushi mat on the table. Place one nori sheet half on the mat horizontally. Dip your hands in cold water, shake off the excess, then scoop up a quarter of the sushi rice. Spread the sushi rice over the nori sheet to cover it evenly. Spread the rice so the surface is relatively smooth but do not press down on it too hard.

Lay about a quarter of the avocado slices over the rice. If the avocado slices are not long enough, make sure the far side of the rice is covered with the avocado, leaving a gap nearest to you, if necessary. Cover the entire surface with cling film. Place another bamboo sushi mat over the top and press it down very gently, otherwise the avocado will get squashed, then turn it all over. Now you have the original sushi mat on the top, so remove this mat.

Mix together the mayonnaise and wasabi paste, if using, then spread a quarter of this over the centre of the nori sheet. Lay the fillings (first 15g of the flying fish roe, then a little shredded lettuce, and finally 2 tempura prawns) horizontally across the centre of the nori sheet, making sure the prawn tails are sticking out either side of the nori sheet.

Using both hands, pick up the side of the sushi mat and cling film closest to you with your index fingers and thumbs. Carefully roll up the nori sheet (using the bamboo mat and cling film as a guide to do this), enclosing the filling (but not the cling film) inside the nori sheet as you roll, rolling away from you towards the far side. Try to roll as tightly as possible, otherwise the fillings can quite easily come out (as the nori is enclosing and holding the fillings together, not the sticky rice). When rolled up, hold the sushi mat around the roll with both hands and squeeze and pat it gently to firm and shape the roll.

Leave the nori roll, seam-side down, on a chopping board for at least 3 minutes, so that the seam in the nori will become glued naturally. During this standing time, the nori will shrink slightly, therefore it's important to rest it for a few minutes before cutting.

Repeat with the remaining ingredients to make a total of 4 rolls. Cut each roll into 8 slices before serving.

NIGIRI-ZUSHI

(HAND-MOULDED SUSHI)

300g cooked sushi rice (see recipe on
   page 35)
toppings of your choice, such as
   pieces of raw fish (see Cook's Tip)
wasabi paste, to taste (optional)

This style of sushi really depicts the art of sushi. Many years of training are required to master the technique of making nigiri. It has to be beautiful to look at, but at the same time the rice has to be firm enough to hold the fish, yet light enough for you to enjoy every bite.

Usually raw fish are the toppings for hand-moulded sushi, or sometimes sweet egg omelette or cooked peeled prawns can be used. Each hand-moulded piece of sushi should be about the size of a dessertspoon – the rice ball is about the size of a ping-pong ball (which is then moulded into a slightly oval shape) and the topping (typically fish) is about 5mm thick.

SERVES 4 (MAKES 20 PIECES)

For each piece of sushi, dip your hands in cold water, scoop up about 1½ tablespoons sushi rice (each rice ball should weigh about 15–20g), then gently but firmly mould the rice into a ball, making it slightly oval in shape. Do not squash the rice but make sure the grains stick together firmly. The size of the rice ball must be smaller than the toppings. Repeat with the remaining sushi rice to make about 20 rice balls.

Place a little fish topping on top of each rice ball and press them lightly together (spread a little wasabi paste in-between the topping and the rice, if you like). The fish topping should be elegantly draped over the rice. Serve.

COOK'S TIP
Fresh tuna and salmon are the most popular fish to use for this dish in the West, but other fish such as sea bass or sea bream, can also be used. The fish should be sliced into 5mm-thick slices, each about 4 x 2cm in size (each prepared piece of fish will weigh about the same as each rice ball – about 15–20g).

DUCK NIGIRI

SERVES 4
(MAKES 20 PIECES)

Prepare the recipe for Seared Duck Breasts with Soy Balsamic Sauce (see recipe on page 166), omitting the deep-fried leeks, then cool the cooked duck and sauce to room temperature (the cooled sauce should be thick – like the consistency of condensed milk).

Follow the recipe for Nigiri-Zushi (see page 202), using the duck breast as the topping instead of the fresh fish. Garnish each duck-topped rice ball with a little grated (peeled) fresh root ginger and finely chopped spring onions, then drizzle the thick sauce over the duck and serve.

TOMAGO NIGIRI

SERVES 4
(MAKES 20 PIECES)

Prepare the recipe for Tamago-Yaki (see recipe on page 56). While the cooked egg mixture is still warm, roll up the egg omelette using a sushi mat to help, then leave a small plate on top of the omelette roll for 10 minutes to press it down. Cut the omelette diagonally into 6mm-thick slices, so that the size and shape will be perfect for topping the rice balls.

Cut a nori sheet (about 19–20cm square) into 20 long ribbons (12–14cm long), each about 1cm wide. Top each rice ball with an omelette slice, then wrap each omelette-topped rice ball in a ribbon of nori, making sure the two ends of the nori ribbon meet underneath. There is no need to stick the ends of the nori ribbon together as they will naturally stick together from the moisture and weight, if you leave them for 20–30 seconds. Serve.

GUNKAN NIGRI

(Hand-Moulded Battleship)

The word 'Gunkan' directly translates as 'battleship'. Usually non-solid topping ingredients, such as fish roe, sea urchin, etc, that cannot be laid on top of the rice in one piece, are served this way. Modernised and more economical versions of toppings include tuna mayonnaise, sweetcorn mayonnaise, prawn cocktail and so on. Use your imagination for the toppings to create your own versions.

Cut nori sheets (each sheet about 19cm square) into ribbons or strips, each about 10cm long and 2.5cm wide. Make as many nigiri rice balls as you require, following the Nigiri-Zushi recipe on page 202.

Wrap a nori strip around the outside of each rice ball, gently moulding the rice ball and nori into an oval shape – like a battleship. Make sure the top edge of the nori comes up a little higher than the top of the rice, so that the toppings can easily be held in place on top of the rice. Lean the assembled 'battleships' against each other so the ends of each nori strip stick together.

Using a teaspoon, spoon the chosen filling(s) on top of each rice and nori 'battleship' and serve immediately, otherwise the nori will become soft and the 'battleships' will quickly lose their shape.

CHIRASHI-ZUSHI

(COLOURFUL SCATTERED SUSHI)

10 medium dried shiitake
   mushrooms
3 tablespoons caster sugar, plus 1
   teaspoon caster sugar
500ml warm water
1 large carrot
200g canned bamboo shoots
   (drained weight), drained
2 sheets of deep-fried tofu (about
   20g each)
110ml cold water
110ml soy sauce
2 tablespoons sake
2 tablespoons mirin
a little vegetable oil, for frying
3 eggs, beaten with a pinch of salt
80g mangetout
a pinch of salt
8 good-quality crabsticks, 8 thin
   slices smoked salmon or 8 cooked
   peeled tiger or king prawns
2 tablespoons toasted sesame seeds
600g cooked sushi rice (see recipe on
   page 35)
pickled ginger, drained, to garnish
   (optional)

Put the dried mushrooms in a bowl, add 1 teaspoon sugar and pour over the warm water. Leave to soak for 2 hours, then drain, reserving the mushrooms and 220ml of the soaking water separately. Cut the carrot and bamboo shoots into 10 x 2cm chunks. Blanch the deep-fried tofu sheets in a pan of boiling water for about 30 seconds. Drain well. Set aside.

Chirashi-zushi is often eaten at home in Japan as it is easy to prepare and perfect for a buffet-style meal. It also makes a great accompaniment for a barbecue, just like a rice salad!

SERVES 4

Put the cold water, remaining 3 tablespoons sugar, the soy sauce, sake, mirin, mushrooms and reserved mushroom soaking liquid in a saucepan and bring to boil. Add the carrots, bamboo shoots and deep-fried tofu, then turn the heat down to a simmer and cook for about 30 minutes or until the cooking liquid is reduced by about one-third. Remove from the heat and leave to cool.

Heat a little vegetable oil (about 1 teaspoon) in a small frying pan over a high heat. Pour about one-third or a quarter of the beaten egg mixture into the pan, spreading it very thinly all over the pan base. Cook for about 10 seconds, then quickly turn it over and cook for a further 10 seconds. Tip the omelette out onto a chopping board. Repeat this to make 3–4 very thin omelettes. Make sure the pan is very hot and use a little oil for each omelette, otherwise the omelettes will stick to the pan. Leave the cooked omelettes to cool, then slice them as thinly as possible.

Blanch the mangetout in a pan of boiling water with a pinch of salt added for 30 seconds, then rinse under cold water, drain well and leave them to cool. Once cool, cut the mangetout diagonally into thin sticks. Cut the crabsticks, smoked salmon or cooked prawns into bite-size pieces.

Remove the mushrooms, carrots and bamboo shoots from the cooking liquid. Squeeze the mushrooms (to remove excess liquid), then cut them into long and very thin slices. Finely chop the carrots and bamboo shoots.

Add the carrots, bamboo shoots, deep-fried tofu, sesame seeds and half of the mushrooms to the sushi rice in a bowl and mix them together gently, adding the cooking liquid from the vegetables as you go. Mix well.

Cover the rice with the omelette slices and top these with the remaining mushrooms, the mangetout and seafood (arrange the toppings over the rice so that they are all visible – the dish will be very colourful). Garnish with a little pickled ginger, if you like, and serve.

TUNA AND SEA BASS GOMADARE (SESAME SAUCE) CHIRASHI-ZUSHI

160g fresh tuna (sashimi-quality)
160g fresh sea bass (sashimi-quality)
2 tablespoons soy sauce, plus extra
    to serve
2 tablespoons mirin
1 teaspoon sesame oil
1 tablespoon toasted and ground
    sesame seeds
4 shallots
10 shiso leaves
80g watercress
1 avocado
800g cooked sushi rice (see recipe on
    page 35)
2 tablespoons black sesame seeds
wasabi paste, to taste, plus extra to
    serve

Chirashi-zushi is the most popular way to eat sushi at home as it is easy to prepare. You can substitute with other sashimi-quality fish or even cooked meat or vegetarian options.

SERVES 4

Slice the tuna and sea bass into bite-size pieces. Mix the soy sauce, mirin, sesame oil and ground sesame seeds together in a large bowl. Add the tuna and sea bass pieces to the marinade and mix well to coat the fish all over. Set aside for about 5 minutes.

Slice the shallots and shiso leaves very thinly. Tear off and discard any thick stalks from the watercress. Halve, stone and peel the avocado, then roughly chop the flesh into 2cm cubes.

Put the sushi rice into a large serving bowl, add the shallots, shiso leaves, watercress, avocado pieces and black sesame seeds and mix together gently.

Place the marinated tuna and sea bass on top of the sushi rice mixture with the marinade. Place a little wasabi paste on top of the fish. Serve with extra soy sauce and wasabi paste on the side.

COOK'S TIP
If you prefer, you can serve the sushi rice mixture in individual serving bowls (dessert or soup bowls are ideal), then place the fish, marinade and wasabi paste on top of each portion, dividing evenly.

DESSERTS

GREEN TEA ICE CREAM

350ml double cream
350ml soya milk or full fat milk
1 egg
2 egg yolks
180g caster sugar
1 tablespoon green tea powder
3 tablespoons boiling water

This is the most popular Japanese dessert in the West. It combines a slight bitterness from the green tea with the sweetness of custard to create a well- balanced and delicious ice cream.

SERVES 6

Heat the cream and milk together in a saucepan until hot, but not boiling. While the cream mixture is heating, whisk the egg, egg yolks and sugar together in a large bowl.

Put the green tea powder in a cup, pour over the boiling water and stir until the mixture is smooth, making sure there are no lumps. Add the green tea mixture to the hot cream in the pan and whisk well until all the green tea has completely dissolved into the cream mixture.

Pour the hot cream mixture into the egg and sugar mixture in the bowl and whisk until thoroughly mixed. Pour the mixture back into the pan and cook over a low heat, stirring constantly with a wooden spoon, for about 5 minutes or until the custard is thickened enough to coat the back of the wooden spoon (see Cook's Tips). Do not allow the mixture to overheat or boil, otherwise it will curdle or scramble (see Cook's Tips).

Pour the custard into a chilled bowl and allow it to cool. As it cools, stir the custard occasionally to prevent a skin forming on the surface. Cover and chill

in the fridge for 1 hour.

Pour the chilled custard into an ice-cream maker and churn until frozen (following the manufacturer's instructions for your particular model). Alternatively, pour the chilled custard into a shallow, freezerproof container, cover with a lid and freeze until firm, whisking the mixture 3 or 4 times during freezing (every hour or so) to break down the ice crystals and ensure an even-textured result.

Allow the ice cream to soften slightly at room temperature or in the fridge before serving.

.

COOK'S TIPS

To test if the custard is thick enough, try to draw a line on the back of the wooden spoon – if the line remains clearly, it is ready; if you can't draw a line in the custard, return the mixture to the heat and cook gently for a few more minutes until it thickens enough.

If the custard starts to curdle, quickly take the pan off the heat, put the pan in a shallow bowl of cold water and whisk the mixture vigorously until it becomes smooth again

AZUKI BEAN ICE CREAM

350ml double cream
350ml soya milk or full fat milk
2 eggs
3 tablespoons caster sugar
120g azuki bean paste (see recipe on page 39)

Azuki bean paste is a traditional Japanese dessert ingredient and it is used in many authentic Japanese desserts. In Japan, azuki ice cream is the most popular flavour alongside vanilla.

SERVES 6

Heat the cream and milk together in a saucepan until hot, but not boiling. While the cream mixture is heating, whisk the eggs and sugar together in a large bowl.

Pour the hot cream mixture into the egg and sugar mixture in the bowl and whisk until thoroughly mixed. Pour the mixture back into the pan and cook over a low heat, stirring constantly with a wooden spoon, for about 5 minutes or until the custard is thickened enough to coat the back of the wooden spoon (see Cook's Tips in Green Tea Ice Cream recipe, opposite page). Do not allow the mixture to overheat or boil, otherwise it will curdle or scramble (see Cook's Tips, opposite page).

Pour the custard into a chilled bowl and allow it to cool. As it cools, stir the custard occasionally to prevent a skin forming on the surface. Once cold, stir in the azuki bean paste until well mixed, then cover and chill in the fridge for 2 hours.

Pour the chilled custard into an ice-cream maker and churn until frozen (following the manufacturer's instructions for your particular model). Alternatively, pour the chilled custard into a shallow, freezerproof container, cover with a lid and freeze until firm, whisking the mixture 3 or 4 times during freezing (every hour or so) to break down the ice crystals and ensure an even-textured result.

Allow the ice cream to soften slightly at room temperature or in the fridge before serving.

BLACK SESAME ICE CREAM

FOR THE ICE CREAM

350ml double cream
350ml soya milk or full fat milk
1 egg
2 egg yolks
80g caster sugar

FOR THE BLACK SESAME PRALINE

160g caster sugar
1 teaspoon cold water
60g black sesame seeds

To make the praline, lay a wide sheet of foil on a cold work surface. Put the sugar in a heavy-based pan and heat gently until the sugar has melted, tilting the pan to melt the sugar evenly. Do not stir or mix. When the last bit of sugar is about to melt, add the cold water and gently swirl the pan to combine the melted sugar and water. Add the sesame seeds and tilt and shake the pan, making sure all the seeds are well coated with the caramel. (Do not try tasting the mixture at this stage as it will be very hot and will burn your lips and tongue!) Quickly pour the sesame mixture onto the foil, spreading it evenly so that it is no thicker than 3mm (it will be about 20 x 20cm in size). Leave the praline to cool and harden, then peel off the foil.

Sesame seeds work surprisingly well in this sweet, creamy ice cream. If you prefer, toasted white sesame seeds can be used instead of black ones.

SERVES 6

Make the ice cream. Heat the cream and milk together in a saucepan until hot, but not boiling. While the cream mixture is heating, whisk the egg, egg yolks and sugar together in a large bowl.

Pour the hot cream mixture into the egg and sugar mixture in the bowl and whisk until thoroughly mixed. Pour the mixture back into the pan and cook over a low heat, stirring constantly with a wooden spoon, for about 5 minutes or until the custard is thickened enough to coat the back of the wooden spoon (see Cook's Tips in Green Tea Ice Cream recipe on page 212). Do not allow the mixture to overheat or boil, otherwise it will curdle or scramble (see Cook's Tips on page 212).

Pour the custard into a chilled bowl and allow it to cool. As it cools, stir the custard occasionally to prevent a skin forming on the surface.

Break up the sesame praline into small pieces, then crush them into a finer crumble-like texture using a pestle and mortar or a food processor.

Once the custard is cold, stir in the crushed praline, mixing well, then cover and chill in the fridge for 1 hour.

Pour the chilled custard into an ice-cream maker and churn until frozen (following the manufacturer's instructions for your particular model). Alternatively, pour the chilled custard into a shallow, freezerproof container, cover with a lid and freeze until firm, whisking the mixture 3 or 4 times during freezing (every hour or so) to break down the ice crystals and ensure an even-textured result.

Allow the ice cream to soften slightly at room temperature or in the fridge before serving.

WHITE MISO ICE CREAM

350ml double cream
350ml soya milk or full fat milk
125g white miso paste
1 egg
2 egg yolks
200g caster sugar

This is the most innovative ice cream I have ever made. The saltiness and sweetness of white miso paste creates a yet undiscovered and joyful flavour.

SERVES 6

Heat the cream and milk together in a saucepan until hot, but not boiling. Add the miso paste and stir until the miso paste has melted completely. While the cream mixture is heating, whisk the egg, egg yolks and sugar together in a large bowl.

Pour the hot miso cream mixture into the egg and sugar mixture in the bowl and whisk until thoroughly mixed. Pour the mixture back into the pan and cook over a low heat, stirring constantly with a wooden spoon, for about 5 minutes or until the custard is thickened enough to coat the back of the wooden spoon (see Cook's Tips in Green Tea Ice Cream recipe on page 212). Do not allow the mixture to overheat or boil, otherwise it will curdle or scramble (see Cook's Tips on page 212).

Pour the custard into a chilled bowl and allow it to cool. As it cools, stir the custard occasionally to prevent a skin forming on the surface. Cover and chill in the fridge for 1 hour.

Pour the chilled custard into an ice-cream maker and churn until frozen (following the manufacturer's instructions for your particular model). Alternatively, pour the chilled custard into a shallow, freezerproof container, cover with a lid and freeze until firm, whisking the mixture 3 or 4 times during freezing (every hour or so) to break down the ice crystals and ensure an even-textured result.

Allow the ice cream to soften slightly at room temperature or in the fridge before serving.

GREEN TEA BRULÉES

3 teaspoons green tea powder
3 tablespoons boiling water
360ml double cream
220ml full fat milk
4 large egg yolks
240g caster sugar

As green tea is a very popular flavour in Japan, it is used in many different desserts. As well as green tea ice cream, these brulees are another simple Japanese dessert. It is best to make and bake the egg custards the day before and leave them to chill overnight in the fridge before you caramelise the tops and serve.

SERVES 6

Put the green tea powder in a cup, pour over the boiling water and stir until the mixture is smooth, making sure there are no lumps.

Preheat the oven to 140°C/fan 120°C/Gas Mark 1. Put the cream and milk in a saucepan and bring to the boil. Once the cream mixture starts to boil, reduce the heat to a simmer and add the green tea mixture to the pan. Stir until both mixtures are well combined. Remove from the heat and cool for a few minutes.

While the cream mixture is cooling slightly, whisk the egg yolks and 120g of the sugar together in a large bowl.

Pour the hot cream mixture into the egg and sugar mixture in the bowl and whisk until thoroughly mixed. Pour the mixture back into the pan through a fine colander or sieve, then cook over a low heat, stirring constantly with a wooden spoon, for 2–3 minutes to warm the mixture up (this will help to shorten the cooking time in the oven). Do not let the mixture boil.

Pour the mixture into 6 individual ramekin dishes, dividing it evenly. Place them in a roasting tin, then pour enough warm water into the roasting tin to come two-thirds of the way up the outside of the dishes. Place the roasting tin in the oven and cook for about 30 minutes or until the egg custards are set in the centre (the cooking time will depend on the depth of the ramekins). To check if they are cooked, try gently pressing the centre of each dessert with your finger – if the egg custard is set enough, your finger will spring back.

Remove from the oven, then remove the ramekins from the roasting tin and leave to cool, then refrigerate overnight.

Take the ramekins out of the fridge an hour before serving. Just before serving, cover the top of each egg custard completely with the remaining sugar, dividing it evenly. Caramelise the sugar by either using a blowtorch or by placing the ramekins briefly under a very hot grill until the sugar is melted and caramelised. Remove from the heat and leave to stand for a few minutes (or for up to 30 minutes), then serve.

WHITE MISO SOUFFLÉS WITH GINGER CARAMEL SAUCE

FOR THE SOUFFLÉS

30g unsalted butter, softened
10 tablespoons caster sugar
350g crème patissière (see recipe on
    page 38)
100g white miso paste
1½ tablespoons calvados or brandy
8 egg whites

FOR THE GINGER CARAMEL SAUCE

100g granulated sugar
120ml double cream
6 large slices (peeled) fresh root
    ginger (about 20g in total)
about 1 tablespoon cold water

Make the soufflés. Preheat the oven to 190°C/fan 170°C/Gas Mark 5. Grease 6 x 300ml ramekins with the softened butter. Sprinkle 1 tablespoon caster sugar into each ramekin and tilt each dish so that the inside becomes fully coated with the sugar. Tap out any excess sugar.

Warm the crème patissière in a bowl, either placed over a pan of simmering water for about 7–8 minutes, or in a microwave oven on LOW (about 30% power) for about 4–5 minutes. With either method of heating, make sure the crème patissière does not boil. Stir in the miso paste until it is completely melted, then add the liquor and mix well. Remove from the heat.

This is another innovative dessert I have created. The white miso paste adds an unforgettable and delicious flavour to these soufflés, which are ideal for a dinner party dessert.

SERVES 6

Whisk the egg whites in a clean bowl (preferably not a plastic one) until soft peaks form. Gradually add the remaining 4 tablespoons sugar, whisking constantly. Whisk until the mixture becomes stiff and glossy.

Using a spatula or metal spoon, stir half of the whisked egg whites into the crème patissière to loosen it, then gently fold in the remaining whisked egg whites. Pour the mixture into the prepared ramekins, dividing it evenly. Run your thumb through the soufflé mixture around the inside rim of each ramekin.

Place the ramekins in a roasting tin, then pour enough warm water into the roasting tin to come two-thirds of the way up the outside of the dishes. Place the roasting tin in the oven and cook the soufflés for 15–17 minutes. (Once cooked, the soufflés should be well risen and slightly wobbly. To check, insert a skewer into the centre of one soufflé – it should come out slightly moist but not wet.)

While the soufflés are cooking, make the ginger caramel sauce. Put the granulated sugar in a heavy-based

saucepan and heat gently until melted. Once melted, stir gently over a low heat until it becomes dark golden in colour. While the sugar is melting, put the cream and ginger slices in a separate pan and heat gently until boiling, then simmer for 5 minutes.

Gradually add the cream mixture (in 3 batches) to the caramel, stirring constantly and making sure each batch is well mixed before adding the next. Remove from the heat. The consistency of the sauce should be like condensed milk – if it is too thick, stir in a little cold water; if it is too thin, return the pan to the heat and cook a little more until the sauce thickens to the right consistency.

Set the sauce aside until the soufflés are ready. Remove and discard the ginger slices just before serving and pour the sauce into a small bowl to serve.

Remove the soufflés from the oven. Serve immediately with the ginger caramel sauce alongside.

CREPES JAPONAISE

(AZUKI BEAN PASTE PANCAKES WITH GINGER CUSTARD SAUCE)

200g plain flour
2 eggs, beaten
500ml full fat milk
50–80ml cold water
50g butter, melted
1 ripe medium mango
100g stem ginger in syrup (drained weight), drained
2 tablespoons syrup from the jar of stem ginger
3 egg yolks
25ml sake
a little vegetable oil, for greasing (if your pan is not non-stick)
about 200g azuki bean paste (see recipe on page 39)

Just like the ice creams in this chapter, you can also enjoy Japanese flavours in this Western-style dessert. Azuki bean paste is a traditional Japanese dessert ingredient and it is a great match with pancakes!

SERVES 6

Sift the flour into a bowl, add the eggs and 300ml of the milk and whisk together until smooth and well mixed. Gradually add enough cold water, mixing until the batter is the consistency of double cream. (The crepe batter should be quite runny, not like an American pancake mixture.) Stir in the melted butter. Cover and refrigerate for 15–20 minutes.

Meanwhile, peel and stone the mango and cut the flesh into 1cm dice (make sure you remove all the flesh from the sides of the stone too). Set aside.

Chop the stem ginger very finely, then put it in a bowl with the ginger syrup and egg yolks and mix together well. Heat the remaining 200ml milk and the sake together in a heavy-based saucepan until hot, but not boiling. Pour the hot milk mixture over the egg yolk mixture in the bowl, stirring constantly, then return the mixture to the pan. Heat gently, stirring constantly, for about 3–4 minutes or until the sauce thickens slightly (do not allow the mixture to overheat or boil, otherwise it will curdle). Remove from the heat and keep warm.

Heat a crepe pan or a non-stick frying pan over a medium heat, then carefully grease the pan by wiping it with a piece of kitchen paper dabbed in vegetable oil (you should only need to grease the pan if your pan is not non-stick). Pour in just enough batter (about one-sixth) to thinly coat the bottom of the pan, tilting the pan to spread the batter evenly. Cook for about 1 minute or until little bubbles appear around the edge. Turn the crepe over and cook the other side for 1 minute or until golden. Remove the cooked crepe to a plate lined with greaseproof paper and keep hot. Repeat this process until all the batter is used up (making a total of 6 crepes), stacking the cooked crepes on top of each other with greaseproof paper in-between each one.

To serve, for each crepe, lay it on a chopping board and spread some azuki bean paste over the crepe. Roll up the crepe and cut it in half diagonally. Place the two halves (criss-cross to each other) on a plate, spoon some diced mango alongside and pour over some ginger custard sauce. Repeat for each crepe until all the crepes, azuki bean paste, mango and ginger custard sauce have been used up. Serve.

MONT BLANC

(CHESTNUT TART)

435g can chestnut purée
100g caster sugar
200ml double cream
250g crème patissière (see recipe on page 38)
one baked cold 24cm sweet shortcrust pastry case (see recipe on page 39)

The Japanese love French desserts and this is one of the most popular ones.

SERVES 6

Put the chestnut purée in a bowl and loosen by stirring it with a fork or whisk. Stir in the sugar. In a separate bowl, whip the cream until it forms stiff peaks. Fold the whipped cream into the chestnut mixture, mixing well.

Spread the crème patissière evenly over the bottom of the pastry case, then pipe the chestnut mixture decoratively over the top. You can pipe the chestnut mixture in any design you like (the easiest way is just to pipe rosettes over the entire surface of the tart), although in Japan, this tart is always decorated with long thin lines of piped chestnut mixture to resemble noodles. Serve.

COOK'S TIP
If you don't have time to make the pastry case, you can either use a ready-made shop-bought pastry case, or use a ready-made plain sponge cake instead. To use a sponge cake, simply spread the crème patissière over the sponge cake (or cut the sponge cake horizontally in half and sandwich the two halves together with the crème patissière), then pipe the chestnut mixture over the top of the cake.

JAPANESE MEALS AND MENU PLANS

As food has become a bigger part of people's everyday lives in the UK, more and more people entertain friends by holding dinner parties or get-togethers at home.

The introduction of many international cuisines has spread across the globe and as people have become more interested in and knowledgeable about other cuisines, many want to cook these international dishes at home. But once the dishes have been mastered, one aspect people may struggle slightly with is how to plan a typical menu for a particular cuisine, and this also applies when cooking Japanese dishes at home, or indeed, when eating out at a Japanese restaurant in the West.

I often see people ordering mismatched dishes and too many different kinds of dishes at Japanese restaurants in the UK. Japanese people at home do not eat sushi, yakitori and tempura together in one meal, as they all fight against each other to be the main dish.

JAPANESE MEALS

Casual or everyday Japanese meals at home are often served buffet-style with a balanced selection of meat, fish and vegetables, as well as a combination of textures including soft, crunchy and soup-like Chinese-style dishes.

Other types of typical meals in Japan include a 'Bento Box', which contains several small dishes in one box (the box has divisions inside it). Soup is usually served with it. Originally 'Bento Box' was a lunch box, traditionally made by your mother or wife, but its use has developed more widely over the years and Bento boxes are readily available in many places throughout Japan. This style of meal can also be served as a smarter, slightly more upmarket meal and for this a large, luxurious (often hand-crafted) lacquered box (usually black and/or red) is used to hold the dishes. Either one of these tends to be served for lunch. If the dishes are intended for a child's lunch box then the Bento box used is often colourful and plastic.

Additionally, Bento boxes that are specific to different regions in Japan are sold at main railway stations throughout Japan and their contents vary, depending on the locality. These Bento boxes contain regional food made with regional ingredients and many people enjoy these meals as they travel on the trains.

The most traditional and smart style of meal in Japan is called 'Kaiseki' and this is the equivalent to a tasting menu. Normally about 6-12 small dishes are served, one by one, in a Kaiseki meal, but this type of meal is only served in Japanese restaurants or for special occasions such as weddings, big birthdays or anniversaries. Most Japanese people do not serve this style of meal at home.

As for the dessert, Japanese people usually don't eat anything heavy after their meal and often just have fresh fruits, ice cream, jelly or sorbet as a dessert. All those beautiful cakes, tartlets and pies you see in Japan are normally eaten for afternoon tea.

MENU PLANS

I have arranged the following menu plans by considering the cooking method, so that you don't use your entire collection of pans for one meal, and I have chosen dishes that can be prepared so that the oven and grill are not used at the same time. Some of the cold dishes can be prepared in advance to serve with the freshly cooked, more complicated dishes.

Here are my suggested Menu Plans...

EASY DINNER FOR TWO

Sesame Crumbed Prawns (page 106)
or
Kakiage (page 98)

Steamed Chicken with Sesame Sauce
(page 113)
Cold Soba Noodle and Prawns
(page 76)
or
Ginger Pork (page 71)
Prawn, Cucumber and Wakame Salad
(page 51)
Plain Rice (page 34)

Main course should be served with a
simple miso soup (page 43)

ROMANTIC DINNER FOR TWO

Salmon Carpaccio (page 47)
or
Scallops, Prawns and Shiitake
Mushrooms with Ginger (page 66)

Beef and Vegetable Rolls, served with
Tamago-Yaki (page 69)
or
Seared Duck Breasts with Soy Balsamic
Sauce (page 166), served with Spinach
with Gomadare Sesame Sauce
(page 38)

Main course should be served with
Takikomi Gohan, served with a simple
miso soup and pickles (pages 80 and 43)

VEGETARIAN DINNER FOR TWO

Tofu Steak with Mushroom Topping
(cook without bacon) (page 180)
or
Ganmodoki Tofu with Ginger Clear
Broth (page 179)

Beetroot, Asparagus and Mozzarella
with Tama-Miso (page 153)
or
Tamago-Yaki (page 56) served with
Hijiki Seaweed with Deep-Fried Tofu
and Carrots (page 97)

Somen Noodles with Spicy Aubergines
(page 79)
or
Miso Zosui (without bacon) (page 82)

CASUAL (BUDGET) DINNER PARTY	SMART DINNER PARTY	DECADENT DINNER PARTY
Kakiage (page 98) *or* Gyoza (page 93)	Selection of Sushi (mixture of compressed and rolls will be easy to prepare) (pages 190–209) Agedashi Dofu (page 83) *or* Clear Soup with Minced Chicken Balls (page 91)	Beef Tataki with Creamy Sesame Sauce (page 162) *or* Seared Tuna with Soy-Onion Vinaigrette (page 145)
Miso Marinade Salmon (page 60) Green Beans and Fishcakes with Spicy Mayo (page 100) Japanese Coleslaw (page 55) *or* Ginger-Flavoured Meatballs with Sweet and Sour Sauce (page 108) Broccoli with Miso and Sesame Sauce (page 94)	Buta-Kakuni (page 165) *or* Sake-Kasu Black Cod *or* Miso Black Cod (page 156) Tofu Shiraae Salad (page 150) *or* Calamari and Bamboo Shoot Salad with Spicy Miso Dressing (page 154)	Agedashi Dofu (page 83) *or* Prawn Cakes in Clear Broth (page 142) Scallops with Creamy Spicy Sauce on Sushi Rice (page 141) *or* Salmon Tartare on Sushi Rice with Wasabi Mayonnaise (page 171) Monkfish and Porcini with Citrus Ponzu Soy Sauce (page 159) *or* Miso Marinade Lamb with Miso Blue Cheese Sauce (page 168)
Japanese Potato Salad (page 99)		
Main course should be served with Cold Soba Noodle and Prawns (page 76) *or* Takikomi Gohan (page 80)	Main course should be served with plain rice and pickles	The last course should be served with green vegetables or salad of your choice

CASUAL (BUDGET) BUFFET PARTY

Sesame Crumbed Prawns (page 106)

Tamago-Yaki (page 56)

Nanban Mackerel (page 103)

Chicken 'Tatsuta-Age'-style (page 110)

Ginger-Flavoured Meatballs with
Sweet and Sour Sauce (page 108)

Broccoli with Miso and Sesame Sauce
(page 94)

Takikomi Gohan (page 80)

Lei-Men (page 128)

SMART BUFFET PARTY

Kakifulai with Spicy Ponzu Sauce
(page 146)

Salmon Carpaccio (page 47)

Beef Tataki with Creamy Sesame Sauce
(page 162)

Steamed Chicken with Sesame Sauce
(page 113)

Buta-Kakuni (page 165)

Cha-Soba Noodle and Calamari
with Yakumi Sauce (page 175)

Tuna and Sea Bass Gomadare
Chirashi-Zushi (page 209)

Saba Oshi-Zushi (page 190)

MIXED VEGETARIAN AND NON-VEGETARIAN BUFFET PARTY

Assorted Mixed Vegetarian and
Non-Vegetarian Sushi (page 187)

Sea Bass and Prawn Tempura
with Ponzu Sauce (page 63)

Yakitori (page 72)

Beef and Vegetable Rolls (page 69)

Deep-Fried Tofu with
Black Sesame Paste (page 131)

Nasu Dengaku (page 48)

Beetroot, Asparagus and Mozzarella
with Tama-Miso (page 153)

Tofu and Avocado Salad
with Wasabi Dressing (page 86)

SUPPLIERS

ARIGATO

48-50 Brewer Street,
London, W1R 3HN
Tel: 020 7287 1722

ATARI-YA

Finchley Branch
595 High Road
North Finchley
London, N12 0DY
Tel: 020 8446 6669

Acton Branch
7 Station Parade
Noel Road
London, W3 0DS
Tel: 020 8896 1552

Golders Green
15-16 Monkville Parade
Finchley Road
London, NW11 0AL
Tel: 020 8458 7626

Kingston Branch
44 Coombe Road
Kingston upon Thames
Surrey, KT2 7A
Tel: 020 8547 9891

CLEARSPRING LTD

19A Acton Park Estate
London, W3 7QE
Tel: 020 8749 1781

FUJI FOODS

167 Priory Road
London N8 8NB
Tel: 020 8347 9177

HELLO KITCHEN

10 NorthEnd Road
Golders Green
NW11 7PH
Tel: 020 8209 3414

JAPAN CENTRE FOOD SHOP

14-16 Regent Street
London, SW1Y 4PH
Tel: 020 3405 1246

JAPANESE KITCHEN

(delivery service only)
9 Lower Richmond Road
London, SW15
Tel: 020 8788 9014

MINAMOTO KICHOAN

44 Piccadilly
Westminster
London, W1J 0DS
Tel: 020 7437 3135

NATURAL NATURAL

Finchley Branch
1 Goldhurst Terrace
London, NW6 3HX
Tel : 020 7624 5734

Ealing Common Branch
20 Station Parade
Uxbridge Road,
Ealing Common W5 3LD
Tel : 020 8992 0770

RICE WINE SHOP

17 Air St, Westminster,
London, W1 B5.
Tel: 020 7439 3705

T.K TRADING

(delivery service as well)
Unit 7 The Chase Centre
8 Chase Road
London, NW10 6QD
Tel : 020 8453 1743

INDEX

W

Y

ACKNOWLEDGEMENTS

I am filled with the greatest joy and sense of achievement for finishing this, my first book. *Hashi* represents my whole life. I would like to thank a few people for supporting me along the way and enabling me to reach to this stage.

First of all, a thank you to my mother, and for her dedication to feeding her family well-balanced and freshly-cooked food throughout all the time of my growing up in Japan. She routed a true love of food in me, and it is an appreciation that has blossomed over the years.

It is the same appreciation that I am passing onto my two sons, Tom and Jack. For the past 22 years of my life, my mission and priority has been to create tasty, healthy and fresh food for them. They inspire me greatly. Now grown up and away at university, it remains one of my biggest pleasures to produce for them a Japanese feast each time they return home.

Thanks are also due to my father, who allowed my mother to dedicate her time and passion towards food and pass it on through me.

And big thanks also to my greatest friend, Michelle, who has always been at my side, encouraging me whatever the challenge.

It is, then, to these very special people that I most wish to say thank you: Okaa-san (mum), Otou-san (dad), my boys and Michelle.

And last but not least, I would like to thank everyone at Absolute Press – Jon Croft, Meg Avent, Matt Inwood and Claire Siggery – for such a fantastic job in putting this book together, in time for my very special birthday in 2011.